Where There is Greed . . .
Margaret Thatcher and the Betrayal of Britain's Future

WHERE THERE IS GREED ---

Margaret Thatcher and the Betrayal of Britain's Future

GORDON BROWN

MAINSTREAM
PUBLISHING

To the constituents of Dunfermline East
who have more reason than most
to look forward to the end of the Thatcher era

Copyright © Gordon Brown, 1989

First published in Great Britain 1989 by
MAINSTREAM PUBLISHING COMPANY (EDINBURGH) LTD
7 Albany Street
Edinburgh EH1 3UG
ISBN 1 85158 288 2 (cloth)
ISBN 1 85158 233 9 (paper)

British Library Cataloguing in Publication Data
Brown, Gordon, 1951–
Where There is Greed: Margaret Thatcher and the Betrayal of Britain's Future
1. Great Britain. Politics, 1979–1989
I. Title
320.941

Printed in Great Britain by Dotesios, Trowbridge, Wiltshire

Contents

Foreword

This book is written from Scotland, where government ministers talk incessantly about 'an economic transformation', 'the regeneration of Scottish enterprise' and about economic prospects that are the 'best in our lifetime'. In one speech alone the Prime Minister announced that 'Scotland is on the march again' and 'changing before our eyes' with 'investment that has soared', in a 'soundly based dynamic economic revival' and 'enjoying greater prosperity than anyone in the UK outside the South East'. And all this under a government that 'has liberated the energies of the Scottish people'.

'The Scottish miracle did not happen by accident,' Mrs Thatcher has told us. Our problem is that it has not happened at all. To the 269,000 unemployed Scots, the 500,000 who depend on Giro cheques, the 800,000 on the margins of poverty and the 1.6 million in a nation of 5.1 million who live in what are officially described as 'low income households', talk of economic miracles rings hollow.

And even for those whose standard of living has risen over the last ten years there are anxieties. Pollution, congestion, the rundown of investment in education and health, the various consequences of a neglected infrastructure and the erosion of many liberties combine to produce a real deterioration in the quality of life.

Anyone looking ahead from the Seventies at Scotland's prospects for the Eighties as the oil flowed in would surely have hoped for more. Yet in the ten best oil years Scotland's economy grew 50% more slowly than Britain's southern triangle. Less people are at work now than in 1979. Manufacturing investment has fallen by 14% and even the high technology industries that should have compensated for the rundown of traditional industries have suffered from under-investment, government neglect of education and training and the lack of a coherent national research and regional policy. And all the government has to offer is opt-out schools, opt-out hospitals, and the wholesale selling-off of housing estates and more privatisation generally.

But Scots have lost something else besides. Within days of Mrs Thatcher's coming to power hopes of a Scottish Assembly were betrayed. A majority referendum vote was ignored, the promise that ministers would bring forward new proposals was forgotten and all-party talks on devolution, also pledged, never took place.

Through the Eighties ministers listened less and less. The Scottish Select Committee, which monitors the government's work in Scotland, was abandoned. Whitehall solutions for private health and education were applied insensitively where distinct and separate traditions had previously flourished. The Scottish Office lost power and influence. Scotland became a laboratory of social engineering, with the Poll Tax, a formal abnegation of the concept of fairness, being exacted as this book goes to press.

In Scotland Mrs Thatcher has always governed without support. The reasons, already obvious in Scotland, are becoming apparent in the rest of the country: the economic misjudgement, the social injustice, the environmental neglect, the erosion of highly regarded and previously adequate collective provisions, and the dogmatic refusal to contemplate anything other than private-sector solutions. It is these matters that this book addresses.

My first debt of gratitude is to all my colleagues in the Shadow Cabinet and in the PLP who first raised many of the issues addressed here and on whose advice I have drawn. I am also grateful for the help and advice of a large number of very busy people, many of whom read and commented upon earlier drafts: Victor Anderson, Iain Begg, Tony Blair MP, Dr Jeremy Bray MP, Marion Caldwell, Alastair Campbell, Stanley Clinton Davies, Ken Coutts, Alistair Darling MP, Barry Delaney, John Eatwell, Murray Elder, Steve Eldsworth, Professor Wynne Godley, John Hills, Stephen Joseph, Roger Lawson, Ruth Lister, Lord Irvine of Lairg, Mo Mowlam MP, Deborah Mattinson, Dr Lewis Moonie MP, Peter Mandelson, John McInnes, Neil McKinnon, Chris Paradine, Joyce Quin MP, John Rentoul, Freda Stack, Holly Sutherland, Jack Straw MP, Dennis Turner, Terry Ward, Dave Wheeler. In particular I

FOREWORD

am grateful to Iain Begg, Ken Coutts and Professor Wynne Godley for their advice on the economic chapters. I have also received help from the Shadow Cabinet Economic Secretariat, the Labour Party Research Department, NCCL, NIESR, Friends of the Earth, Greenpeace, The Low Pay Unit, Shelter, John Appleby of NAHA and the staff of the stastical section of the House of Commons Library. I am grateful to Joe Haines for his advice, to Ann Barratt and Jonathan Todres for administrative help and to Rhona White and David Stoddart for all their support.

This book has been a team effort. Without Sandy Hunt and Paul McKinney who work with me in the House of Commons this collection could not have been attempted. I am grateful to Sandy Hunt who has researched and organised most of the chapters, whose expertise in such a wide range of areas is second to none, and whose patience and forebearance is much appreciated And I am grateful to Paul McKinney who coordinated much of the work of the book researching some chapters, operating under the enormous pressure of a tight deadline. What is good about this book is due to their superhuman efforts to organise the disorganised.

My publishers at Mainstream, Bill Campbell, Peter MacKenzie and Anna Fenge, exhibited every virtue ever expected of publishers.

Dr Colin Currie kindly read all my drafts and made helpful comments. Any remaining split infinitives are entirely my own.

This book is dedicated to my friends in Dunfermline East Labour Party and to the constituents of Dunfermline East who have more reason than most to look forward to the end of the Thatcher era.

Introduction

'Where there is discord may we bring harmony. Where there is error may we bring truth. Where there is doubt may we bring faith. Where there is despair may we bring hope.'

When the Thatcher era draws to its close it will be re-evaluated with speed and disbelief. People will look back in amazement at the claims made on its behalf — an economic miracle, a social transformation, a political revolution, an industrial resurgence, the rebirth of Britain — and will very quickly begin to see the 1980s as a decade not of achievement but of missed opportunity.

Historians may agree or disagree about how and why Mrs Thatcher retained power for so long but the crucial question that this book will address is whether, after ten years of Tory rule, Britain is better equipped to face the challenges of its future. In the new global economy, with its world marketplace, its instant communications, its international division of labour and its shift to high value added goods and flexible patterns of production, Britain can no longer survive, far less prosper, on the simplicities of Mrs Thatcher capitalism. Ever lower labour costs, and ever delayed investment, will not be enough to keep us in business as a nation.

In the Nineties, countries will be judged by the quality of their workforce and their investment in skill and technology, and by the responsiveness of their industries and governments to the challenge of continuous evolution in methods, products and markets. Quite simply, if Britain is to do even moderately well over what's left of the 20th century and on into the 21st, the determining factor will be our competitiveness in a world of technology-driven products, of custom-built goods and of precision items where the premium is not just on individual innovative and entrepreneurial flair but also on the skills, adaptability and collective efforts of us all. And all that will necessitate a greater role for organised and supportive interventions by the state.

There is nothing either revolutionary or retrogressive about that. Our more successful international competitors — Japan, West Germany, France and now Italy — are already investing more in education, science and industry; training their workforces better; pursuing innovations and developing them for the market more effectively than we are; and are doing so with a far larger contribution from the state.

Yet for a crucial decade the Thatcher government has not only failed to prepare our economy for the 1990s but failed to advance our quality of life in the Eighties. Living standards have, of course, risen as they have in every decade, but in the Eighties they rose because of the availability of the oil wealth, and more slowly than in countries like Italy which did not have oil. As the decade ends, the three principal objectives that were common ground between politicians of all parties for nearly 40 years have been abandoned: the commitments to full employment, to an acceptable minimum income and to balanced regional growth.

And Britain moves out of the Eighties more congested, more polluted, more rundown and more divided than anyone looking ahead from the beginning of the Eighties would ever have dared to predict. As this book shows, our world trading position has declined, our growth rate has been disappointing, our education, science and industrial investment have stagnated and our unemployment has been intolerable. In the regions and inner cities the suffering that was to be a brief precondition of our economic success has become permanent and that promised economic success is further away than ever.

No other Common Market country had the £120 billion in oil wealth that Mrs Thatcher had at her disposal. No country enjoyed the balance of payments advantage that it brought, the £76 billion taxation revenues it bestowed, the additional growth potential — equivalent to a substantial yearly increase in our living standards — it offered. Oil made us richer but our children will look back and learn with astonishment that despite the huge windfall of North Sea oil it was not Britain but her competitors who in the Eighties invested for the future. Britain, they will be told, actually invested a smaller share of its national income in itself during the oil years than it did in the poorer decade that preceded them.

Poverty runs deeper and wider in our society. Much of our country is congested, grubby and run down. Our schools and hospitals decay and are hastened haplessly from public service to the uncertainties of a make-believe market. Our welfare and social security provisions, once envied, are year by year falling further behind the norms of Europe. A new official secrecy bears down upon the freedom of the press and the individual.

The argument of this book is that Mrs Thatcher's failures are rooted as much in doctrinaire prejudice as in her inability to see beyond the short term. The blind conviction that all Britain's shortcomings in the latter decades of the 20th century can be attributed to the over-reaching state is central to her beliefs.

For Mrs Thatcher, every public effort and provision is suspect. Her economic insights revolve around a naïve yearning for the Arcadian simplicities of a marketplace untainted even by the sinister insights of the historical Adam Smith. She has chosen to apply to the problems of a complex late 20th-century economic scene nostrums devised for an older, simpler world of unspoiled markets, a golden age that probably never was.

Of course the market can and does allocate resources efficiently in many areas, and of course public authority can be bureaucratic and unresponsive. But just as the market is not always right, public intervention is not always and by definition wrong. Yet for Mrs Thatcher it always is, and our future is the more uncertain as a result.

Only by combining public with private intervention, not to suppress the market or dictate to it for reasons of dogma, but to ensure that its forces serve public objectives, can we succeed. That is because the market on its own cannot cope with the complex problems of coordination for the long term that our industrial economy now faces. The market cannot, unaided, educate and train our workforce, plan and fulfil national research goals or restore or even compensate for our battered infrastructure. And the market, unregulated, tends inevitably towards socially undesirable ends such as pollution, inequality and monopoly.

In 1979 Britain wanted change. Voters did not blame the most significant economic event of the decade, the trebling of oil prices and its impact on living standards, for the problems they faced. Instead, they blamed the government, the collective institutions, public spending and the welfare state. No one was more forthright than Mrs Thatcher in

3

arguing that the public sector had failed to deliver the goods and that corporatism was inappropriate for the new economic environment of the 1980s.

The Seventies ended to the sound of the now familiar Thatcher litany: too much public spending, too much red tape, too much bureaucracy, too much taxation and too much government intervention. But if the public wanted a government that would tackle shortcomings within the public sector by seeking to promote greater accountability, responsiveness and flexibility, it was to discover that Mrs Thatcher's plans were different. She wanted to eliminate the public sector entirely from whole areas of national life.

Her aim was 'breaking the shackles on the market'. For too long, Mrs Thatcher claimed, the private sector had been 'held to ransom' by the public sector. For her, any collective public provision, anything that did not arise from the unleashing of market forces and therefore from the profit motive, was inefficient and unworkable. Hers was the pursuit of the Hayek dream of human improvement by unrelieved competion, the flight from the Friedman nightmare of degradation by the nanny state.

For the Prime Minister society revolved around those 'ambitious to make money. Yes — and what's wrong with that?'. Budgets were praised not so much because they helped the poor but because they were a 'spur to the strong'. Lord Young, her favourite minister, applauded the Victorian entrepreneurs who made money 'even at the expense of the poor'. The ideals of service, professionalism, compassion and concern clearly do not mean as much. Indeed as Prime Minister, Mrs Thatcher has given less priority to extolling inventors or exporters, or achievements in sports or the arts, or the professionalism of, for example, teachers or doctors. What she admires is the making of money. As her speeches reveal, the Thatcher heroes above all others have been the Freddie Lakers, the Richard Bransons, the Gerald Ronsons, the Ralph Halperns and the Lord Hansons.

This support for individual acquisitivism colours even her view of individual rights, which are seen to stem not so much from citizenship as from property and wealth. 'There is no prouder word in our history than freeholder,' said Mrs Thatcher in 1982, invoking a direct historical connection between property and rights. Her objective was that 'every family should have a stake in society', not, it seems, as birthright, but by

4

INTRODUCTION

property. Property, she proclaimed, 'brings independence . . . brings freedoms. The great political reform of the last century was to enable more and more people to have a vote,' she told the Conservatives in 1988. 'Now the great Tory reform of this century is to enable more and more people to own property.'

Not the right to health, the right to education, the right to work. For 30 years all political parties had accepted that individual freedom, economic opportunity and social security went hand in hand, that individual rights were best guaranteed by full employment and by the protection of the welfare state. Now Mrs Thatcher argued that many freedoms and rights are to be purchased, and that the welfare state and public provision are the enemies of freedom, true freedom springing from the application of *laissez faire* economics and the inevitable promotion of inequality. Inequality does not matter to Mrs Thatcher. We should not spend our time listening to those 'drivelling and drooling about care'. 'Neither,' she said in 1975, 'is it necessary to allay any sense of social injustice.'

Public provision, in her view, offers only second-class rights. To 'opt out' into private education or private health care is, for her, a higher aspiration. 'A man must choose,' she told the Conservative Party, 'between paying for his children's education and accepting whatever the state provides'. The abnegation of responsibility implicit in that 'whatever the state provides' is chilling: an underfunded public education system should come as no surprise.

Similarly in health, there was no vision of an NHS open to all and providing the highest standard of care for everyone. What she had in mind was more a safety net for the improvident. 'Those who can afford to pay for themselves should not take beds from others,' she told the House of Commons in January 1989 on the day of the publication of the White Paper on the NHS, clearly distinguishing between one health service for those with a lot of money and the other for those who had little.

In 1987 Mrs Thatcher told the *Woman's Own* that in her view there was no such thing as society, only individuals and families. Perhaps, as with her explosion on 'drooling and drivelling' about caring, the moment was an unguarded one, but all the evidence of her actions before and since suggests that it was deeply revealing.

The vision of the society in which she does not believe is a bleak one.

5

Men and women in it buy and sell, are consumers in the marketplace or individuals in perpetual competition with one another. Private health plans, private schools and privatised social services will cater for all their private needs and greeds. It is a world of selfish objectives and therefore of selfish choices.

Yet, as we show in the chapters that follow, on the economy, on education, on the environment and on consumers, it is only by acting as a community that the individual and his rights can be properly protected against the power of vested interests. Without collective action and provision, equality of opportunity is a hollow promise, safer and stronger communities an impossibility, protection for the consumer an illusion and forward planning for our industrial future a vain hope. The successive chapters of this book will show how the government, by failing to act on behalf of the community, has failed that community.

The first five chapters show how Mrs Thatcher has failed to use the opportunities offered by oil to prepare our economy for the challenges it now has to meet. Only supply side intervention — in education and training, in innovation and in technology support, and in enhanced long-term investment — can achieve this. As these chapters show, the huge one-off bonus of North Sea oil, money that could have been spent on equipping a generation of young people for a working life in the post-industrial age, went instead on paying it the dole. There was no coherent national programme of education and training, so skill shortages are with us already while millions of people are being kept expensively idle, under-educated and unskilled.

In innovation and design too we are lagging behind. Mrs Thatcher's naïve faith that the key to progress will be found by a lone inventor burning the midnight oil in his garage has had the effect of denying us a properly funded national programme of research, an advantage most of our competitors enjoy. And generally it is this neglect of investment — in industry and in infrastructure as well as in education and technology — that has characterised the Thatcher years.

As the chapters on the environment, privatisation, consumer rights and inequality argue, the Thatcher experiment has elevated acquisitiveness and indifference to the wider community to the neglect of consumer and employee interests and to the detriment of our quality of life. While assuring us that business always knows best and markets work most efficiently when least regulated, government ministers have abandoned their responsibilities to impose controls in the interests of customers, consumers and the environment.

Inevitably, in the drive towards the unfettered operation of the marketplace, there has been a huge transfer of resources from the poor to the rich, because without the countervailing power of government to help them the weak fall victim to the strong and the many to the greed of the few. Individuals and individual rights suffered accordingly. The failure to tackle various forms of pollution illustrates this.

Ministers will not act to improve investment to purify our water to the highest standards required while they are intent only on privatising it. They will not raise food standards to the quality necessary for fear of offending a vast and, to them, generous food lobby. They will hesitate before tackling safety in consumer goods or even safety at sea because they depend for support on the huge industrial conglomerates. Commercial interests support the Conservatives and the Conservatives support commercial interests.

Chapter 8 shows how privatisation has not enhanced competition or improved services to consumers, and how the main beneficiaries have not been large numbers of small shareholders, many of whom have not stayed the course, but the small number of large shareholders and the hugely rewarded executives. City institutions have made huge windfall gains, and all this has been supported by a tax policy the main objective of which was the biggest ever transfer of wealth and power to the richest few in Britain.

Chapters 11 to 13 show how millions of citizens lost out as a result. Not just in relative but in absolute terms Britain's poorest citizens have become worse off in the oil years. According to reliable European figures we now have far more and worse poverty than we had in the Seventies. Low pay is widespread and becoming still commoner, the more so because wage protection is being withdrawn. Britain's unemployed have been out of work longer and fared worse financially than those in most major European nations. The living standards of men and women on the basic pension lag behind those of old people in other more generous nations abroad. Meanwhile our regions have been abandoned to market forces and many of our inner cities have been described by impartial observers as being outside the mainstream of economic life. None of these problems are being seriously addressed by Mrs Thatcher.

As the chapter on women shows, the whole aim of Mrs Thatcher's family policy has been to make women the reserve army of labour both in the workforce and in the home. And as the government withdraws from responsibility for the poor and the less fortunate, charity has reappeared after 40 years, to play an essential role in our social security system. The most outstanding feature of the Thatcher years is not the dispersion of income among the many, but the concentration of wealth amongst the vested interests of the few.

Yet the Eighties have not seen any mass support for Thatcherite values. There has been no ideological sea-change, no enduring transformation of national attitudes of the kind sought and claimed by the present Tory party. Support for the NHS is undiminished, as it is for the collective provision of education at all levels. Studies tell us that the NHS and the welfare state generally enjoy more support than they did even in the Seventies. The truth is that Mrs Thatcher holds power in spite of Thatcherism rather than because of it. Social justice has not been deserted by the public, just temporarily shouted down by its government.

In their less acquiescent moments many government ministers admit this. Not just Peter Walker but others have questioned the values which underpin the government in which they serve. Sir Geoffrey Howe has said, 'we still have a long way to go in tackling social tensions created by generation gaps, social differences, class and regional differences'. Mr Douglas Hurd has written of the need to 'bring back social cohesion to our country'. And Viscount Whitelaw, still Mrs Thatcher's Deputy Leader, has conceded that 'a little more compassion is needed'.

The central tenets of Labour's social philosophy have always been popular, that people see themselves as citizens participating in a community, not just as buyers and sellers, lonely competitors in a gigantic and impersonal marketplace. People know that individuals on their own cannot make the streets safe at night; that consumers on their own, however enterprising, cannot buy their way out of urban squalor or countryside pollution; and that for a whole range of needs and services collective action and the public spending on which it depends is the most efficient and effective way of guaranteeing these important freedoms. People understand too that only by the community asking to ensure research and innovation skills and training, regional and inner city development and investment and balanced growth generally will our

8

industrial economy flourish. It is true that support for public intervention is not so much ideological as purely practical, and depends on the positive benefits that flow from the NHS, local authority services and economic action, but most people support our commitment to fairness and greater equality, to neighbourliness and strong communities, and to full employment and an economy run broadly in the interests of the community at large.

The public are not opposed to our values: the challenge for Labour is to demonstrate that our policies adequately reflect them. It has of course always been easy to misrepresent socialism. Our best defence against this is to spell out our commitments in practical terms and show how we will open doors and break down barriers as we empower people with new rights and opportunities. As a starting point that means modern policies for affordable homes, for child care, for high standards in schools, for retraining instead of redundancy for employees shouldered out of jobs, for a clean environment and most of all for creating pathways out of poverty for millions of low paid workers and poor households whom this government has forgotten.

In the 1940s a minority of citizens paid taxes to support our public services. Now a majority do and if we are to show how collective provision and public investment work for the British people we must not only champion fair taxes but also demonstrate clearly that socialists are wise and efficient spenders rather than, as the Tories would have it, just big spenders. In the provision of both public and private sectors accountability, efficiency and choice must be guaranteed. In the Health Service, as elsewhere, diversity and decentralisation — not least through legislative devolution in Scotland and Wales — should be the guiding theme. And in dealing with private sector cartels, many so dominant that they can fix prices at the expense of the consumer, a broader array of weapons should include full rights to information, to high-quality service, to quick redress of grievance including financial penalties and refunds where the service is poor.

But it is how we plan for a successful economy that will determine whether we are recognised by the broad mass of the public as their natural voice in government. At its best socialism has always been concerned with production and not only distribution, with our basic case that unbridled capitalism is inefficient as well as unfair and economic intervention not just moral but more productive. Current economic trends in the new global marketplace — the international division of labour, the shift to high value added specialist goods, the flexible patterns of production — reinforce this case. As later chapters seek to show, the Tory obsession with top rate tax cuts has blinded them to the real supply side measures we need if Britain is to compete successfully. Our competitors do not believe that national salvation can be achieved by their governments screwing public spending down to a minimum and relying on the scientific genius and entrepreneurial skills of lone inventors working in garden sheds. They recognise the purposeful role government can play as catalyst and coordinator. Infrastructure for them is a matter of continuing responsibility and continuous updating. They have followed industrial strategies that have accepted the necessity of extensive research and development nationally encouraged and nationally funded. Most of all they recognised that investment in education and training, and indeed in the personal well-being of their workforces, is more vital than ever to economic success. A campaign to make Britain the world's best educated and best trained nation will promote social justice: it is also essential to our economic performance. Efficiency and fairness depend on each other.

In this way a new supply side socialism for Britain is in the making. Its main themes are investment in skills and science, with teamwork, collective effort and the involvement of the workforce vital to a successful economy. Socialism has always been about more than equality, with political and social rights fragile and incomplete as long as they existed side by side with huge concentrations of private unaccountable power. Our task is to forge a strong economic democracy in which people can realise their full potentials, secure the fruits of their labour and play a large part in shaping the decisions that affect their working lives. In the new economy of the Nineties, as we escape from the malign simplicities of Tory dogma, that goal is within our grasp.

Preparing for the Future?

I

The Miracle That Never Was

'Many other governments are now Thatcherite . . . my performance against that of other countries in the real world is such that the majority of them are following us and not us following them.'

Mrs Thatcher, 1984

In March 1988 the Chancellor, Nigel Lawson, told the House of Commons that 'the country is now experiencing an economic miracle comparable in significance to that previously enjoyed by West Germany and still enjoyed by Japan'. Yet after a full decade of North Sea oil revenues Britain's economic performance has not begun to emulate or even remotely approach that of Japan, the boasts of Mr Lawson and Mrs Thatcher notwithstanding. On every major indicator, as Table 1 shows, Japan has outpaced and outperformed Britain over the last ten years.

Our manufacturing production has grown by less than 8%, Japan's by 41%. Industrial production has now risen by 10% in Britain but by 43% in Japan. Exports, up by 86% in Japan, have risen by 28% in Britain. General investment, which has risen by 51% in Japan, has risen by only half as much here. In brief, Japan's economy has grown twice as quickly: its exports have increased almost three times as fast; its industrial production has risen four times as fast; and its manufacturing output five times as fast.

Only the British government has had North Sea oil and all its investment potential. In total Mrs Thatcher's government has had £76 billion in oil revenues, £76 billion available to no one else.

Mr Lawson's miracle has been very modest indeed: so modest that, despite a reduction of unemployment figures by 1 million in 2 years, we

WHERE THERE IS GREED . . .

have still been left with 1 million more unemployed than in 1979, the lowest growth rate over any period of comparable duration since the war, inflation at 8% and interest rates at 13% — both figures the highest amongst our major competitor countries — a balance of payments deficit, still rising from an unprecedented £15 billion, and net manufacturing investment running at one-third of the levels of the previous decade.

Mr Lawson's economic miracle is so modest that in the league table of industrial countries we are falling behind Italy. During the last ten years British economic growth has been slower than that of almost all of our major competitors, slower than that of the Organisation of Economic Cooperation and Development countries as a whole, and slower than the average of the seven major economic powers. While Mrs Thatcher boasts vainly of keeping up with Japan, the harsh reality is that we are slipping gradually down a list that includes countries never before thought of as potential rivals. And while Mr Lawson proclaims that in investment, productivity and growth Britain has been leading the international league, the painful truth, as Table 1 shows, is that in terms not only of growth, production and investment, but also in terms of inflation, interest rates and exports, we are much nearer the bottom. Manufacturing production has grown at only about a third of the rate of OECD countries, and after ten years of Mrs Thatcher, inflation is now nearly twice the OECD average.

Table 1   How the British Economy Compared

1979–1988: % Annual Average Growth

	Gross Domestic Product	Manufacturing Production	Exports	Imports	1988: Balance of Payments % GDP	Total Investment as % GDP	Inflation 1989	Interest Rates 1989
United Kingdom	2.0	0.8	2.8	4.6	−3.1	17.3	7.8	13
USA	2.7	2.6	5.0	5.9	−2.7	17.8	4.4	10
Japan	4.0	3.9	7.2	3.4	2.8	29.4	0.9	4.5
Germany	1.6	1.1	3.9	2.7	3.7	20.5	1.6	6.5
Italy	2.5	1.5	2.9	4.6	−0.5	21.5	4.8	12
OECD	2.5	2.2	4.2	4.3	−0.4	N.A.	4.4	N.A.

THE MIRACLE THAT NEVER WAS

The real miracle, if any, is that all this has been passed off as a success. Astonishingly, that is something Conservative ministers have managed to do, at least for a year or two. They succeeded because at the same time they have squandered rather than invested the oil billions, together with £30 billion of privatisation proceeds. They claim to have succeeded because the shock of their first two years in charge was so great that thereafter almost anything could be made to look like a strong recovery. The miracle has simply been one of deception.

The argument of this chapter is that government mismanagement in areas where they had a direct national responsibility — in fiscal and monetary policy and in supply side measures — has been so great that even when manufacturing industry has managed to achieve productivity gains, the British economy has not benefited as it should have done in the oil-rich years. Not only did the experiment with monetarism produce a disastrous and excessive reduction in industrial capacity in the first years after 1979, but government neglect of their responsibility to encourage investment throughout the 1980s has meant that the capacity was never fully replaced or modernised. The consumer boom they created without investment in the mid-Eighties led to imports from abroad rather than substantially increased production at home. In ten years household consumption increased by 29%, industrial production by only 10.5% but imports by 50%. Ministerial failure to use all the available economic weapons at their disposal to secure balanced growth was matched only by their mishandling of the few instruments they eventually used. As our account of policy decisions over ten years shows, ministers swept through a bewildering array of monetary and other indicators in a manner that was both inconsistent and incompetent.

That failure arose not just from their unwillingness to discharge their responsibilities but from an antipathy towards any form of public intervention in the regions, in stimulating training, in research and investment generally. While masquerading as resolute, ministers subordinated the serious needs of industry to the short-term and speculative concerns of City finance and as a result we enter the more competitive 1990s having failed to address the underlying weaknesses of British industry.

And despite the wealth from oil Britain's performance from 1979 onwards compares unfavourably even with that of its own recent past. Indeed for all post-war ten-year periods before 1979 growth has been higher. It is interesting to note that while under the 1974–79 Labour government growth averaged 2.4% a year, it has averaged only 2% a year from June 1979.

But the greatest economic failure has been the perpetuation of mass unemployment. No boasts about the reduction of the figures over the last year or two can obscure the fact that since 1979 unemployment in Britain has risen by over a million, and has been substantially higher than the OECD average.

The figures quoted for Britain are the official ones, but it has, of course, been government policy to minimise the true unemployment that exists. The plan was quite simple: to define a useful percentage of the unemployment out of unemployment, by a series of measures all of which are essentially fiddling with the statistics. The rules governing the definition of unemployment have been changed on no less than 20 occasions.

Although the initiative directed at the long-term unemployed has generally failed in its overt aim of getting people back to work, it has dented the figures for long-term unemployment because many of those targeted have been dissuaded by one means or another from claiming benefit. Other similar campaigns, against the older unemployed, against single parents and the young, constitute the government's main effort in reducing the unemployment figures.

Despite these dubious campaigns, unemployment remains high, and similarly our record in the creation of jobs is not all that government ministers claim it to be. Britain's achievement in employment creation over the last ten years as a whole compares dismally with most of our major competitors. Total employment between 1979 and 1987 rose by 14% in the USA, and by 8% in Japan, whilst in Britain it fell by 0.3%.

With high unemployment and the shedding of labour has come higher manufacturing productivity. As we entered the 1980s there were many areas where productivity growth was essential. Where these productivity increases have been achieved by advanced technological development and a specific effort by industry they are to be welcomed. Yet where such increases have occurred they have often happened in spite of government policies that have tended to be inconsistent.

The commonest form of growth in productivity that we have seen has been the result of an exercise in the shedding of labour, a slashing of industrial manpower unsurpassed in recent UK and foreign experience.

In many of our manufacturing industries employment has fallen a great deal and output has fallen but less drastically. Increased productivity in that context is simply an aspect of the huge fall in employment.

And whatever its origins, productivity growth under the Tories has remained unimpressive. The economist Gavyn Davies, critically examining the record of the decade, found that early impressions were best. A period of increased productivity, due to the mass shedding of labour, and a period of growth, due to a consumer boom, combined to give an impression of genuine recovery in 1986. This was feared to be unsustainable and in the event not sustained, and in Davies' words, productivity growth in the whole economy has been very disappointing. Productivity over the Thatcher years has gone up by only 1.5% a year, the worst annual average of any ten-year period since the war.

Nor has this increase in productivity in the manufacturing sector been accompanied by any significant increase in production. It brought increased profits, but not increased investment at the level essential for increased competitiveness. The profits have gone instead to higher dividend payments, to funding a wave of domestic takeovers and to financing overseas acquisitions — which will do little to improve our balance of trade.

Since 1979 vast sums have left the country and been spent on purchasing companies abroad: £3 billion in 1979, rising to £14 billion in 1986, £68 billion in all. In 1987 companies spent over £15 billion on takeovers in Britain and by 1988 the figure exceeded £20 billion. This contrasts with an annual average of only £1 billion spent on British takeovers over the five years of the last Labour government, a total of £5 billion from 1974 to 1979. The recent spending on acquisitions is in fact twice that on manufacturing investment and nearly half the total of all company investment.

Many takeovers went ahead despite the absence of any industrial logic. As the *Financial Times* said in October 1988 when highlighting the case of the Hanson Trust, which, it said, had long been operating successfully as a warehouser of businesses, 'in the past year or so it has begun to seem that almost no bidders wanted to buy companies to run them better, but rather to sell off the bits at a profit'.

Yet still a 'supply side miracle' has been claimed. It is a claim that is impossible to justify. Even Lord Young, the government's most publicity conscious spokesman, has been forced to admit that after ten years 'the level of productivity is on average about one-third to one-half of our competitors'.

Nor is the position likely to improve over the coming years. In their study of Britain's experience in the Thatcher years, Layard and Nickell have concluded that 'while there certainly remains a considerable gap in productivity between British plants and similar European plants the evidence suggests that this will start to become more difficult to close because of the comparatively low levels of training embodied in the British workforce'.

Despite the claims of Mrs Thatcher, markets have failed to generate the investment and the related changes that are necessary to bridge the productivity gap. As Professor Nick Crafts concludes in a wide ranging summary of the available evidence 'the upshot is argued to be a slow rate of adoption of new methods and a failure to reap the full potential of technological change. In economic terms these arguments imply widespread market failure in the sense of failure to achieve an efficient allocation of resources. This argument also suggests market failure in the sense that market forces operating through new entry and takeover were not able to prevent an inadequate productivity performance.'

The market failure that Professor Crafts identifies has been compounded by the failure of government, a failure both in macro-economic policy — seen first in the recession of the early Eighties then in the consumer boom of the mid-Eighties — and in micro-economic policy — dealing with the supply side of the economy. In micro-economic policy the failure was to eliminate positive intervention on the part of the public sector in areas such as training, research and regional investment, even when the market had failed to do the job. In macro-economic management, the failure was to rely on crude weapons of policy instead of recognising that the many objectives of economic management require a flexible use of fiscal and monetary interventions.

The policies that have been pursued throughout the 1980s have been crude and unsophisticated in relation to the problems they set out to tackle, namely the complex and interlocking difficulties that modern high techonology economies face in an ever more open marketplace. There was a general failure to take the steps necessary to make the best and most efficient use of all the resources of the British economy, mass unemployment and the neglect of the regions being the obvious examples.

Behind both failures, as we will show, is an unwillingness to use the power of government to assist economic development. What was described by government publicists as 'freeing business' and 'exposing Britain to market forces', was often at best, putting short-term profit-making before long-term considerations more in keeping with our future competitiveness. The consequences for our future have been dire.

Between 1979 and 1981 mismanagement in the form of an overharsh fiscal and monetary policy, a high pound and high interest rates led to the loss of more than 1.5 million manufacturing jobs. When the real problem, the combination of high imports and inadequate export performance, required the response of a coherent industrial strategy, Mrs Thatcher insisted on exposing our industries to the withering blast of a recession. The collapse of output and employment was the worst ever, outstripping that of 1920–22 and far worse than that of the 1930s. At a stroke, 20% of our capacity was wiped out in an unprecedented act of economic devastation.

At the time and later this wholesale destruction of employment was defended in terms of trimming down British industry for its ultimate benefit, of subjecting it to a winnowing process in which the best would prosper and the weakest go to the wall. Recent research, however, suggests that the recession destroyed successful firms as well as uncompetitive ones. The closures included large plants with higher than average productivity. One study has discovered that plants 'tended to be closed in diversified firms while less profitable plants in undiversified firms soldiered on unless forcibly closed by bankruptcy'. Many died not because they were obsolete but because firms sacrificed them from choice, as branch plants in hard times.

Having made one set of mistakes from 1979 the same ministers made another from the mid-Eighties onwards. They engineered a consumer boom which, since it had not been preceded by an adequate preparation of British industry by investment, was bound to end in rising imports, higher trading deficits and the higher inflation and interest rates that ensued. The degree of deregulation that preceded the boom was uprecedented and irresponsible: the entire financial system — consumer credit, banks, building societies and overseas capital movements — was deregulated in such a way that the credit boom and the boom in asset prices drew millions of families into debt.

The growth that resulted did not amount to a supply side miracle: instead it was a demand-side boom, precariously based on speculative credit. The boom was so unbalanced that growth rates in the rapidly overheating southern triangle were twice those of the hard-pressed regions. And for the country as a whole, with consumption growing much faster than production, the inevitable result was that imports rose fastest of all.

The first failure in this ten-year history of economic mismanagement was the government's failure to deploy skilfully and appropriately the various instruments available to it in fiscal and monetary policy. So crude was the government's technique that for long periods it relied on one weapon only in the fight against inflation. The weapon might change, but one and only one was applied at any one time. Monetarism came and went. Control of public spending was briefly enthroned before a return to the crudest, most short-term and bluntest instrument of all, high interest rates.

In 1979 it all seemed so simple. If you controlled the supply of broad money, inflation and all the other problems would solve themselves. With M3 stubbornly doubling instead of falling as planned over the first five years, and still growing at a steady 20%, it is little talked of in Downing Street today. In quick succession the real test of economic health became the now forgotten basket of monetary targets; then the meaningless 'little Mo', which once conveniently fitted the bill; then the total level of public spending, which for electoral reasons had to be hurriedly raised; then the public sector borrowing requirement, blissfully but senselessly excluding any concern about total borrowing; and finally rising interest rates, so attractive to the City but so damaging to industry.

Narrow money had been rejected by Nigel Lawson in his January 1981 speech in Zurich. 'Narrow money has the advantage of being easy to control,' he said, 'but it suffers from being almost too easy to control. In particular a rise in interest rates . . . will inevitably lead to a marked switch from non-interest bearing time deposits thus sharply depressing the growth of narrow money far beyond any true change in monetary conditions.'

But as early as 1983 he was telling a Mansion House audience that MO, narrow money, was the proper test, because other measures of money were unacceptable. The fact was that they had become embarrassing. MO was to become the 'favoured indicator', at least as long as it gave answers that suited the government.

Tories who once thought they possessed a great truth in monetarism came to realise that it had its limitations. As the Governor of the Bank of England was to confess to students at Loughborough University, 'It cannot be said that our experience with our chosen framework for operating monetary policy has been satisfactory.'

There was no evidence that Mrs Thatcher ever understood monetarism anyway. When asked by Peter Jay in a television interview about the monetarist theory of the natural rate of unemployment, the rate of unemployment at which inflation ceases to accelerate, Mrs Thatcher revealed her ignorance by answering with a complete *non sequitur*: 'It is a theory to which I have never subscribed. At the moment, in spite of three and a quarter million unemployed, we have a current account surplus.' Perhaps this is an example of what was meant by the commentator who described her economic insights as 'Hayek for the suburbs, as taught by Sir Keith Joseph but perhaps not fully understood'.

It is instructive to recall that the government thought in 1979 that interest rates, now the sole instrument of economic intervention, could and should be left to the market. By the workings of a kind of economic determinism embodied in monetarism, interest rates would find their level. When the minimum lending rate system was suspended it was 'to allow market factors a greater role in determining the structure of short term interest rates and permit greater flexibility in those interest rates'.

In 1980 it was the stated intention of the Economic Progress Report that 'judgements about appropriate levels of interest rates are replaced by control of the monetary base'. As the report stated the aim was 'a greater role for the market in determining interest rates'. Interest rates were not the means for regulating the economy; an economy regulated by monetarism would optimally determine its own interest rates. As the 1981 Budget report explained, the government was 'committed to a progressive reduction in the growth of the money stock and to pursuing the fiscal policies necessary to achieve this *without excessive reliance on interest rates*'.

The government that repudiated exclusive reliance on interest rates in 1981 is today the government that talks of little else. Now interest rates are not only the government's monetary policy, they are presented as its financial, industrial, trade and even regional policy. Real interest rates are high and have remained high and have been much higher under the Conservatives than under Labour. High interest rates have swung the balance of advantage heavily towards the lender and against the interests of industry, whose borrowing costs have increased by £1.2 billion in less than a year.

Another result is that mortgages are higher. They have been above 10% for 118 months out of the 120 that Mrs Thatcher has been in power. High interest rates, taken together with rising house prices, mean that home owners who in 1979 spent an average of 14% of their income on their mortgages are having to spend an average of 25% now.

The elimination of inflation was the government's professed aim. The Chancellor set the aim as 'zero inflation' in 1984, 1986 and 1987. The record on inflation would be 'judge and jury' of the government's performance. The judge and jury are unimpressed, as Mrs Thatcher approaches her tenth anniversary in power with inflation moving upwards. Inflation is now twice what it was when Mr Lawson became Chancellor, twice what it was a year ago, and much higher than our competitors: Japan is on 0.9%, Germany on 1.6%.

And the government must take responsibility, because, as it is vital to note, 1970s inflation was a product of world conditions, as commodity and oil prices exploded. Inflation was high everywhere. By contrast, in the 1980s, world commodity prices have been stable and oil prices have been generally lower.

Ministers now have no one to blame but themselves. Electricity and water prices have been forced up to make these industries attractive privatisation propositions. Rates, rents, health charges and rail and tube fares have been rising, in some cases at twice the general rate of inflation. Not surprisingly the CBI has complained that 'prices under government control are rising six times faster than those subject to the disciplines of the marketplace. We can do without these inflationary own goals.'

Instead of basking in the promised zero inflation, Britain is enduring the highest inflation rates, the highest interest rates and the worst trade deficits of our group of competitor nations. We have now witnessed the doubling of inflation in a year, nine rises in interest rates in six months and a series of trade deficits accumulating in consecutive months at levels that were once regarded as unacceptable over an entire year.

The authors of this misery remain remarkably impervious to its significance. For Mrs Thatcher and her ministers current inflation is merely a 'temporary blip' on the road to zero inflation, the interest rate rises a transient phenomenon and the balance of payments figures only freak figures that are in any case the inescapable problems of success.

Others take a more hard-headed view of what is happening to the British economy. High interest rates are part of the problem, not part of the solution. A consumer boom without prior, adequate and sustained investment effort was bound to be untenable and, tragically, the very weapon chosen to slow it down, that of high interest rates, will itself discourage future investment.

Once again, because of their antipathy towards any kind of intervention, ministers simply will not take the necessary remedial action: supply side measures to stimulate investment in the regions, in education and research, and to ensure proper balance in the economy. Even when asset sales and oil revenues have brought a budget surplus ministers refuse to use it for investment. Having failed to learn from their mistakes in the mid-Eighties, they seem intent on repeating them over the next few years, using the budget surplus for pre-election top rate tax cuts that will only feed another unsustainable consumer and credit boom.

Nowhere is the irresponsible short-termism, the naïve subservience to free market economics and the inevitable damage it brings to the economy more obvious than in the failure to develop a proper industrial strategy in the approach to 1992. Ministers besotted with the dogma of the free market and contemptuous of the role of government intervention have destroyed the prospects for proper preparation for that harsher marketplace, and instead of strengthening our industries have simply stood aside.

The result is that the implementation of the single European market has been left by default to the Germans and the Italians. The adoption of uniform standards will have major implications for every sector of industry, yet no attempt is being made to come to grips with this. No sector by sector study of the risks and benefits of the single European market is under way. No new training intitiative is proposed to improve skills and even the language facilities to cope with the changed market have been neglected. There are no plans to increase supportive investment or to address the key areas of research, science and technology in a way that will equip industry to meet the new competition on equal ground.

WHERE THERE IS GREED . . .

In short the government ministers aspire to nothing more construc-
tive than simply letting people know the single European market exists.
In the guise of resolution they are supine before the markets, even when
they are visibly failing us. No amount of expensive government
advertising can obscure this central weakness.

2

'Manufacture or Die . . .'

'It has often been said we must export or die. I would add that we must manufacture or die even quicker.'

The author of that clarion call to industry and government was the then Leader of the Opposition addressing the Conservative Industry Conference in 1976. The Rt Hon Mrs Margaret Thatcher was mounting a fierce attack on the fashionable view about service industries, telling us that Britain 'cannot live by them alone' and warning that production was lower even than during the three-day week of 1974 'due principally to the present government's disastrous mishandling of our economy'.

Mrs Thatcher was right about manufacturing industry. It is our ability to produce manufactured goods and compete in our own and in world markets that is central to our industrial and economic performance. Oil has come and is now declining. In 1985, at its peak, it was contributing £8.8 billion a year. Today, with its eclipse, the importance of the underlying deficit in our manufacturing balance of trade is all too clear. It is only in manufacturing that the possibilities of large-scale trade now exists. Many services such as hairdressing, catering and retailing, while of enormous importance in providing employment, cannot be exported, and even those that can, for example insurance and banking, are simply not undertaken, as the Bank of England has confirmed, on a scale that could make good the rapidly growing deficit in manufacturing.

As Table 1 shows, there has been a rapid worsening of our manufacturing trade deficit from 1980 onwards, but there has been no compensating improvement in services. Manufacturing trade has moved from surplus to deficit, worsening by £17 billion since 1979, but the service surplus is not big enough, nor growing fast enough, to make good the manufacturing deterioration. Services, while important to growth, have not filled the trade gap left by the decline of manufacturing exports. As Mrs Thatcher rightly said, 'Britain cannot live by them alone'.

Table 1   Balance of trade in manufacturing, services and oil: 1979–88

(£ millions, current prices)

	Manufactures	Services	Oil
1979	+2,737	+3,907	−685
1980	+5,457	+3,949	+161
1981	+4,584	+3,923	+3,152
1982	+2,371	+2,762	+4,734
1983	−2,264	+3,721	+6,882
1984	−3,878	+3,941	+8,422
1985	−3,001	+5,962	+8,772
1986	−5,701	+5,631	+3,970
1987	−7,508	+5,333	+4,157
1988	−14,440	+3,473	+2,165

It is through manufacturing that we will succeed or fail, and at the moment by any objective criteria we are failing. The reasons are not hard to find. Since 1979 manufacturing imports have grown by 100% while manufacturing exports have grown by only a third.

Fifteen years after the three-day week and ten years after Mrs Thatcher became Prime Minister, the manufacturing production she rightly considered crucial to our economic well-being is only very slightly higher. Only last year did it edge above the 1979 levels and it is now only 7.5% above that year's figure. During that time manufacturing output has grown by 14% in Italy, 26% in the USA and 41% in Japan.

Manufacturing matters for our exports, for our regions and for the creation of the wealth upon which our services depend, yet it is now the weakest link in our economy. Whilst banking and finance have grown by almost 7% a year and distributive trades, services, construction and energy by more than 2%, manufacturing industry has grown by only 0.8% annually.

There is no doubt that a great decline has occurred over huge areas of our manufacturing industry. The question for Britain as it faces the 1990s is whether that decline is now irreversible. Has our capacity dwindled beyond the point of recovery for international competitiveness? Has our industrial emphasis become so skewed towards low technology that we can no longer offer any effective challenge in the big league?

Five years ago the National Economic Development Council reported that our industrial economy was so weak that we were already in a position midway between that of an industrialised nation and an industrialising one. Now that not only Germany, Japan and France, but Italy, Taiwan, Singapore, Hong Kong and Korea are performing better, and Spain is catching up fast, can anything be done to rescue British manufacturing industry?

There is no more telling demonstration of our declining industrial capacity than a look around our shops. Again and again on their shelves British goods are outnumbered and outclassed by imports. Over the past ten years our own markets have been captured by foreign products to a quite astonishing extent. In 1979 less than half our cars were imported. Now the figure is 60%. We now import 40% of our buses and lorries too. In 1979 less than half our black-and-white TVs and only 18% of colour TVs were imported. Now the figures are 100% and 40% respectively. In 1979 only 2% of our telephones came from abroad. Now it is more than 40%.

In newer manufacturing areas we are doing even worse. Microwaves, dishwashers and VCRs, just emerging as mass consumer goods in 1979, are almost all now imported from overseas. For microwaves the figure is 60%, for dishwashers and videos 80%. For computers the proportion of imports is even higher.

But it is not only in consumer goods that we are failing. Last year saw a 22% increase in what are known as intermediate goods — effectively components that will be assembled in Britain but for which the sophisticated high-value part of the production process has been done elsewhere. The final products are not British-made. They are British-assembled: foreign components fitted together in screwdriver plants. Even 'British' goods in our shops now have a high foreign content.

As a result we now import 36% of our manufacturing goods. In 1979 we imported only 27% of them. Imports from Korea and Taiwan have grown by 255% and 372% respectively, and those from Japan by 267%. Japanese imports which in 1979 used to be only 1% of our national income are now 2.4%. But the widening deficit with Europe is even more alarming. In 1979 it was £4.6 billion, rising to £14.6 billion in 1987 and £17.6 billion in 1988. And in the case of just one country, Germany, it rose from £2.5 billion in 1979 to almost £5 billion in 1983 and £7.5 billion in 1987.

Changes in the world pattern of manufacture and trade are inevitable and over the last two decades great changes have occurred. Whereas in the 1960s about 20% of the range of British goods were exposed to international competition now almost every local product has a rival from abroad. But we have not compensated with competitive exports. In no other major country have exports grown so slowly.

If Britain was doing badly in the traditional industries, and its imports concentrated in these areas, then the problem might not be so bad. As traditional industries decline, new high-technology industries might, in the 1990s, take their place. But the reality is that Britain is losing most ground in the high technology industries — information technology, office equipment, chemicals and electronics — on which our future depends.

The failure of British manufacturing industry to keep pace with world developments is illustrated all too clearly in the growth of imports in the high technology, high value-added areas. In low technology manufactures such as textiles, clothing, paper and printing, and food, drink and tobacco, penetration rose from 20% to 30% between 1980 and 1987, while in medium technology manufactures such as metals, shipbuilding and rubber and plastics, the increase was from 26% to 34%. But in the highest technology goods, such as electronics, instruments and specialty chemicals, import penetration, high in 1980 at 41%, has risen to a humiliating 53%. The difficulties we face in all high technology areas are evident from these figures alone.

Table 2   Import penetration

	1980	1987
High research-intensity goods	41%	53%
Medium research-intensity goods	26%	34%
Low research-intensity goods	20%	30%

So poor has been our performance in these high research-intensity areas upon which our competitive future depends that since 1979 our imports in them have almost doubled. If we are to prosper as a nation we will rely on high technology industry to form an increasing part of an expanding economy. The problem for Britain is that high research-intensity goods have not grown significantly as a share of our national income or as a share of manufacturing output. A nation once composed of designers, manufacturers and traders is in danger of becoming a nation at best of assemblers, at worst shop assistants.

Increasingly manufacture is being driven downmarket or into niche products, and Britain is no longer a player in key industries. And without an internationally competitive set of high technology industries Britain will fare badly in the future.

In pharmaceuticals, where Britain should be in the vanguard and where we still have a trade surplus, the growth of exports has not kept pace with imports. In 1980 exports were three and a half times the value of imports, but in 1987 only twice as high. Now there is only one British pharmaceutical company among the world's top 15 by size, and only one among the world's top ten by research effort. And in chemical production we have fallen too, a poor third in Europe behind West Germany and France.

In cars, Britain is now firmly in the second division, with an output only a quarter of that of Germany, and Spain having recently overtaken. In electronics, home-based British companies have grown more slowly (2.6% yearly between 1976 and 1986) than Japanese (7.6% yearly) and American companies (6.6% yearly) also based in Britain. British electronics companies are now among the slowest growing and have failed both in maintaining home markets and in competing effectively overseas.

As the McKinsey report showed, our poor competitive performance is due to inadequate investment in capital equipment, in skills and in research and development. In fact the trade deficits in the newest areas of data processing, electronic components and consumer electronics are now £500 million, £900 million and £800 million respectively. Indeed nowhere is our failure more obvious than in the fastest expanding area of information technology where even Britain's largest company is now only 20th in the world with just 1% of the market. As the all-party House of Commons Select Committee on Trade and Industry pointed out in a major investigation in 1988 'there are many areas in which UK companies have been innovative — for example ICL with content addressable file store, Inmos with the transputer — but despite early technical leads there is no confidence that those products will become world leaders or that similar products will not be more successfully exploited by Japanese or US competitors'.

Their conclusion was that 'the government has no strategy for information technology'. Three-quarters of Britain's basic integrated circuits are already imported. While the information technology market as a whole is expected to grow by 10-15% (the Japanese, for example, forecast that information technology will represent 20% of their national income in 2000), Britain is already losing out. The trade deficit in information technology is already more than £2 billion and rising. Even our more successful companies, like Inmos, once a leading public sector firm, have now been bought up from overseas, on this occasion by a French state company.

One reason why high technology industries find it more difficult to prosper in Britain is because of their recent vulnerability to takeover and merger, and the pressure that is placed on them to achieve short term profits at the expense of long-term investment and research. British industry has always been subject to the whims of the City, but in the last ten years Stock Exchange merger mania has put even Britain's most successful companies at risk.

Funds that should have gone directly into new investment have gone into takeovers, which have, in the words of one expert, Professor John Kay, been 'ludicrously expensive'. British industry has spent ten times as much on fees and commissions for takeover bids alone than on management education in what many see as a negative sum game in which management time and investment bankers' fees represent wasted resources. And the main share gains have not been for solid industrial performance backed by research, innovation, training and investment but have been speculative windfalls during takeover activities. For example share prices rose by 50% during the Hanson takeover of Imperial in 1986, by 50% during the Rank Hovis Macdougall takeover of Avana in 1987, by 167% during the BP takeover of Britoil in 1988 and by 58% during the News International takeover of Collins this year.

There is little evidence that the wave of takeovers has done much for industrial development. A Department of Industry study has highlighted the consistent findings of academic studies that mergers have done little or nothing for efficiency gains. No less a supporter of the government than Sir Hector Lang of United Biscuits has warned that the implications of such takeovers had not been thought through.

Instead of advancing the interests of our successful industries — and making it easier for them to spend on new technologies — the government have, by their monopolies policy, made them more vulnerable to takeovers. Once again competition policy has become subservient to financial interests. Guarantees of company independence, such as the Golden Share protecting Britoil against takeover, have been as quickly abandoned when a predator appears . . . Promises made to government ministers in the heat of takeover bids — such as the Guinness promise to locate its headquarters in Scotland — have been as quickly forgotten and Ministers have refused to ensure compliance. Most worrying of all, government rules on takeovers have been reinterpreted to benefit the speculative bidder. The law states that the public interest should be considered in takeovers and mergers. Mr Norman Tebbitt, while Industry Minister, said that he would use his discretion to consider only competition in individual product markets. In other words, undue concentrations of power, foreign ownership, asset stripping and job losses as well as strategic considerations were to be largely ignored. Lord Young has endorsed this approach. While making noises that he would 'still retain the power to make a reference on public interest grounds' he has repeated that 'competition will be the main consideration in my decision where to refer'. Officially the emphasis is on preventing monopoly in UK markets. In practise since June 1988 Lord Young has had no real concern about 'a larger share in the UK market as long as there is international competition in that market'. His statements are a green light making possible a new wave of takeovers of successful British firms in the run-up to 1992.

But it is the general neglect of investment that explains why our manufacturing industries are finding it difficult to compete internationally or to meet domestic demand. The shrinking of our manufacturing base between 1979 and 1981, together with cumulative underinvestment since, has left us with a capital stock in manufacturing inadequate to meet current needs.

Information from the CBI demonstrates beyond doubt the current predicament of British manufacturing industry. Because of underinvestment a growing number of firms are unable to produce goods for which there is a ready market. The proportion of firms reporting such capacity constraints on their output stood in 1979 at 13%. In 1988, with output hardly any higher, the proportion reporting capacity constraints has doubled to 26%. Clearly there has been a highly significant decline in British manufacturing capacity.

Table 3 shows that under Mrs Thatcher capital investment has grown in volume by 10% in the communications and transport industry, by 24% in private housing, by 44% in the distributive trades and by 123% in the financial and business services while in manufacturing industry it has remained virtually static. A resulting irony is that distributive trade investment has risen dramatically because we are building warehouses to store, distribute and display imported goods on an ever-increasing scale.

Table 3   Investment by selected categories

	1979	1988	% change
	(£ millions, 1985 prices)		
Oil and gas extraction	3,010	1,755	−41.7
Other energy and water supply	3,945	3,835	−2.8
Manufacturing	10,136	9,970	−1.6
Distribution, hotels, catering	4,547	6,554	+44.1
Financial, business services, etc.	5,950	13,320	+123.9
Transport and communications	5,376	5,937	+10.4
Private dwellings	9,665	12,030	+24.5

Net capital manufacturing investment, including leasing, has averaged only one-third of the level achieved in the Seventies, £914 million a year, compared with £2,473 million a year (all at 1985 prices). Cumulatively, compared to the preceding decade, the underinvestment amounts to £14 billion. Even taking gross figures, the underinvestment in manufacturing is staggering. In 1979 Britain invested more in manufacturing than in buying private homes. Today we invest more in buying private homes than we do in our manufacturing industries. Even the nudging up of investment figures in the last two years cannot undo the damage of the previous eight.

Perhaps our poor performance is summed up best in the ever declining British share of world trade, the importance of which is conceded by the government in the claims it has made. 'The sign of our competitiveness is the size of our share of world trade in manufacturing goods. For the first time in decades, under this government, we have maintained our share of exports and world trade in manufactured goods,' the Chancellor has boasted. Mr Alan Clark, the Trade Minister, has said, 'the decimation of our manufacturing industry is pure myth. Since 1981 our share of world trade has remained absolutely constant.'

Unfortunately for the Chancellor and for Mr Clark, the Treasury has provided the House of Commons Library with its own internal assessment of the true position.

Table 4   Manufacturing exports: Britain's share of world trade

	Volume %	Value %
1979	8.2	7.5
1980	7.8	7.8
1981	7.1	6.9
1982	7.3	6.7
1983	6.9	6.1
1984	6.8	5.9
1985	6.8	6.0
1986	6.8	5.7
1987	7.0	6.0
1988	6.8	6.2

In no period since the 1960s has our share of world trade been lower than it has been under Mrs Thatcher. Our share, which was 8.2% by volume in 1979, has fallen successively and in 1988 reached an all-time low of 6.8%. And there is no comfort in turning from figures for volume to those for value. By that measure the fall in our share of world trade has been just as great, from 7.5% to 6.2%, and it still continues. The annual report of the British Overseas Trade Board makes the position quite clear, revealing that Germany, Italy and Japan have all increased their share of world trade while Britain's has seen a significant fall. As imports grow and exports dwindle our situation becomes steadily worse.

Our balance of payments matters. A deficit of more than 3.7% of GDP in 1988 and for the last six months of nearly 5% of GDP means Britain is having to import huge sums of hot money and is at the mercy of currency speculators. Professor Wynne Godley has calculated that, if we continue to run a deficit at this rate, Britain is at risk of using up all its overseas assets and becoming a debtor nation within a decade. No Chancellor who claims to have a medium-term strategy for long-term prosperity should treat such a balance of payments deficit with such cavalier disregard.

Our present huge deficit is of great consequence, however much the Chancellor seeks to deny this. His earlier thinking on the topic is now of some interest. In the 1960s he took it more seriously. 'The peculiar English Sickness,' he said, has been 'our recurrent and steadily growing balance of payments deficit . . . Not least the manifest failure of government measures to solve the overriding balance of payments problem led to disillusionment with governments, politicians and parties in general. There is no need to look any further for the root cause of the growing sense of national malaise.' The balance of payments, he said, 'created the dilemma of being unable to expand the economy as fast as we are physically able because whenever we do imports rise faster than exports'.

Even in 1979 a satisfactory balance of payments in manufacturing was identified as the single most important objective by the then Chancellor, Sir Geoffrey Howe. The story now is very different. Today the deficit is dismissed as 'a freak', 'a problem of success', a problem of 'second order importance', and 'self correcting'. It is said that it doesn't matter because it is a purely private sector phenomenon, the government's own accounts are now said to be in order. The problem is that the present level of domestic demand, whether public or private, is excessive in relation to our ability to produce, even though we still have two million unemployed. The growth of the economy cannot be sustainable unless its ability to compete with foreigners in world and domestic markets is commensurate with the growth of domestic demand whether public or private. It is also said that the deficit is harmless because levels of private investment in Britain are high and that many of the excessive imports are investment goods which will strengthen our long-term position. Leaving aside the issue of whether we should be capable of making our own investment goods, to blame the import of investment goods is to misrepresent the facts.

Imports in consumer goods are growing far faster than those in investment goods. As the unfortunate Trade Minister was compelled to report to the House of Commons, 'Over 70% of the deficit is accounted for by increased consumer spending' (13 July 1988). More and more convincing explanations are required. It is even suggested that the deficit matters less now because of substantial British-owned investments abroad. Alas for government apologists, the benefits of wealth overseas are already accounted for by the inclusion of the dividends from it in the balance of payments.

Other explanations are equally unconvincing. It has been implied that the problems of financing the deficit are really non-existent because in times of difficulty there is sufficient money abroad that could be brought home. This fails to recognise that in a crisis its owners might put money above country and demonstrate their lack of faith in the British economy by keeping it abroad, or repatriating it only at interest rates that would result in great damage to investment.

It is also said that the deficit is a private sector phenomenon which will disappear when the gap between private sector saving and investment closes. Another explanation offered is that the deficit arises because investment here is attractive to foreign owners of capital. Yet direct investment abroad by UK residents exceeded direct investment in the UK by foreigners by £3.9 billion in the first half of 1988. Over that period the net outflow of portfolio investment was £5.6 billion. In other words the inflow is in the form of hot money, drawn here by high interest rates rather than by the prospect of useful long-term investment, and the price of sustaining it will be the continuation of high interest rates. As a recent adviser to the Bank of England writes, to finance a continuing deficit an ever increasing interest rate differential with our competitors is required. As one commentator has pointed out, in these circumstances interest rate rises can become an 'addiction'.

The problems of our manufacturing industries remain, and in these circumstances can only get worse. Our balance of payments deficit arises from poor industrial performance. This results largely from low investment. But to finance our balance of payments deficit high interest rates are required. Because of these high interest rates adequate investment in industry is further off than ever.

3

Investment: Neglect into the Nineties

'There is evidence that the UK's rate of innovation has been falling behind that of its principal competitors. Consequently it appears that the UK now enjoys an intermediate status between advanced industrialised countries and the newly industrialising countries and has features of both types of economy in trade with others.'

*The Director General of the
National Economic Development Council, 1984*

Mr David Marshall: To ask the Chancellor of the Duchy of Lancaster which Overseas Economic Co-operation and Development countries spend (a) a larger and (b) a smaller share of their gross domestic product on fixed investment than the United Kingdom.

Mr Alan Clark: Comparisons for most OECD countries are readily available only for 1986. In that year the following OECD countries spent a larger share of the GDP on fixed investment than the United Kingdom: Australia, Austria, Canada, Denmark, Finland, France, Germany, Iceland, Ireland, Italy, Japan, Luxembourg, Netherlands, New Zealand, Norway, Portugal, Spain, Sweden, Turkey and the United States.

Belgium spent a smaller share of GDP on fixed investment than the United Kingdom. Comparable figures for other OECD countries are not available.

Hansard, 11 May 1988

If Britain is to succeed in the world marketplace of the future it will be in the field of high value-added, custom-built, technology-driven products. This effort depends above all on investment. The lesson of the Eighties is that Britain has failed to make the investment at the level that is necessary. A year or two's nudging up of the investment figures does not compensate for a huge shortfall extending over almost a decade.

Over the Eighties and despite all the opportunities that arose from North Sea oil we have invested a smaller share of our national income than in the Sixties and Seventies when we were poorer. We have also invested a smaller share of our national income than our main competitors — Japan, Germany, France, Italy and America. We have even invested a lower proportion of our income than Portugal, Greece and Turkey, as ministers had to admit when tackled in the House of Commons. As Table 1 demonstrates, since 1979 only Belgium has been investing as small a share of its national income as the United Kingdom. If, since 1979, we had invested as big a share of our national income in our future as France we would have invested £115 billion more, if as much as Italy £160 billion more, and if as much as Japan, or even Korea and Taiwan, £400 billion more.

Table 1   Gross Fixed Investment as % of GDP

Selected periods

	1960–73	1974–79	1980–84	1985–89
Belgium	21.6	21.9	17.7	16.8
Denmark	23.8	22.1	16.7	18.5
Germany	24.9	20.8	21.1	19.6
Greece	22.4	22.8	21.0	18.5
Spain	24.0	24.6	20.9	20.4
France	23.5	23.4	21.2	19.3
Ireland	20.7	25.9	26.0	18.2
Italy	26.0	24.6	22.6	20.3
Luxembourg	26.0	25.1	23.8	21.2
Netherlands	25.0	21.0	19.0	19.8
Portugal	24.0	26.3	28.7	24.4
UK	18.3	19.3	16.8	17.9
EUR	23.2	22.2	20.5	19.4

Source: European Commission Annual Economic Report

Industrial investment has been poorest of all. In 1989 manufacturing investment has only just crept back towards its value in 1979. In every single year under Mrs Thatcher until 1988 the real value of that investment has been lower than in the year she took power. Net manufacturing investment averaged £2,473 million under Labour. It has averaged only £914 million under the Conservatives. Nor has our investment performance compared favourably with other countries. Manufacturing investment fell by 15.6% between 1979 and 1986 in Britain but rose by 1% in Italy, 7% in France, and 17% in Germany. Where the cumulative investment up to 1986 formed only 62% of the value added in British manufacturing in 1986, it was 65% in Italy, 79% in Germany and 92% in France.

One telling example of the neglect of investment is in the automation of our factories. Britain is falling behind Japan, Germany, America and even Third World competition. In machine tools, the main indicator of shopfloor investment, we are doing particularly badly and are now behind both Italy and France. According to the Machine Tool Trades Association £700 million was spent on metal working machine tools in 1979. In 1988 the value of investment, after adjusting for inflation, was only £500 million. Since 1979 overall machine tool purchases have risen by only 10% at home, while in France, Italy and West Germany they have risen by 100%. The fastest growth of all has been in Spain.

In 1987 West Germany spent nearly £3 billion in total on all its machine tools, while Britain spent only £670 million. Italy spent more than £1 billion and France £750 million. Britain has made some progress in numerically controlled machine tools — only 18% in 1979, and 37% now — but still lags far behind its main competitors. Germany has done best, ahead of us in every area: the volume and spread of automation, the use of flexible machine tool cells, robots and material handling systems like conveyors and automated guided vehicles. Germany now installs as many new robots every year as there are robots in place in Britain.

Where automation investment has occurred it has been concentrated most in the processing trades, in chemicals, in paper and food and drink. Investment in engineering has been particularly weak, with the result that the *Financial Times* has reported that 'in terms of closing the technology gap with West Germany the past few years have been little short of disastrous'.

Investment is the key to the rejuvenation of traditional industries which can survive and expand only if they adopt new products and new processes. Our textile industry could and should be enjoying a technology-led resurgence but investment in new spinning and weaving equipment lags behind Europe's biggest producers, Italy and

INVESTMENT: NEGLECT INTO THE NINETIES

Germany. 90% of ring spinning machines in Britain are more than ten years old, compared with only 50% in Italy. 70% of our yarn is produced on machinery more than ten years old, compared with Italy's figure of 29%. Only 25% of our looms use modern shuttle-less tubes, compared with 44% of Italy's and 46% of Germany's.

Our investment failures can be explained at least in part by the way our industries are financed. There is in Britain little tradition of industrial banking. Retained earnings have financed most of the physical investment carried out by British industrial companies. High interest rates have not and will not encourage companies to borrow from outside.

The difficulty for Britain and its economic future is that even when the government has had to acknowledge that such investment as has taken place is mainly for replacement, rather than for renewal and re-equipment with new technologies for a world market, the same government simply refuses to recognise that inadequate investment is a problem at all. Even when ministers knew that our investment was much lower than our competitors, capital allowances were withdrawn with nothing to replace them. Although the investment gap is huge the government refuses to help industry bridge it. From the 1940s to the end of the 1970s public investment made a large contribution to our economic and social well-being, responsible for anything between 2.8% and 4.8% of our national income. Since 1979 the share of public investment has fallen below 2% in almost every year. Even when account is taken of council house sales the share of public investment in the last year for which full figures are available is only 1.67% of GDP. British public investment is not only at a post-war low but it compares very unfavourably with public investment elsewhere in Europe.

Table 2   Public Investment as Share of National Income 1987

Britain	1.9%
France	3.1%
Germany	2.4%
Japan	6.9%
Canada	2.3%
Sweden	3.5%

The neglect of public investment and of investment generally shows how shortsighted and narrow the government approach is. If the

39

British government had made the same contribution to investment as our competitors then up to £20 billion more of our oil revenues would have been used during the 1980s to bridge the huge investment shortfall.

The Tory argument is that jobs, prosperity and international trading success come from one source and one source only: the thrifty and energetic individuals who start businesses, generate profits and subsequently invest them to create more jobs, prosperity and success. The truth is that, welcome as the development of new businesses is, such endeavour represents only a part of the real economy in the real world.

In the real economy there are no virtues of private investment that are not also the virtues of all investment, public as well as private. In the real economy government investments are as important to long-term business development in the private sector as company profits. In the real economy the public organisation of infrastructure, and of education, training and research, is crucial to the welfare of the economy. As the CBI has pointed out, 'There is no sense in industry tooling itself up for the 21st century if workers are inadequately trained, if it is not prepared to develop new products and if the supporting public infrastructure is not there.' It is to the need for, and the current neglect of, effort in these vital areas that we now turn.

Central to our industrial future is investment in research and development where, as things stand, only £1 is spent on innovation in British industry for every £1.50 spent in Germany and Japan. As Mr John Banham of the CBI has said, 'at present we are falling behind in the one race we cannot afford to lose if we are to sustain the standard of living to which we aspire'.

Important as it is to our industrial performance today, research will be even more important in the future. No longer is the business of innovation a once and for all breakthrough in new designs or products. In the new global economy where nearly everyone has access to the machines and the money to turn new ideas into standardised mass products it will be those countries which are in the business of continuous innovation, transforming new ideas into incrementally better products that are tailor-made for customers, that will do best. The changing international economy requires us to move up the quality ladder with sophisticated and specialist high technology research such as putting standard components together in unique ways to create communications systems designed for one company, or incorporating specialised software with standard hardware.

In this way competitive advantages will come from continuous improvements. These demand collaborative work and collective effort by properly funded teachers or researchers, not just in the laboratories but at the point of production itself. The countries that will do best are those where there is least divide between the laboratory and the factory floor, between the highly qualified group of research scientists and the workforce on the assembly line. But as the Director General of the National Economic Development Council warned in 1984, 'there is evidence that the UK's rate of innovation has been falling behind that of its principal competitors. Consequently it appears that the UK now enjoys an intermediate status between advanced industrialised countries and the newly industrialising countries and has features of both types of economy in trade with others.'

As the December 1988 European Commission report on research and development makes clear, there is an obvious need for us to step up and intensify new research on information technology and telecommunications, in industrial materials, in aerospace, in biological sciences and in energy. Britain and Europe need to master and develop the next generation memory chips and the information technologies generally; keep pace with the vast changes in the electronic components sector, including optoelectrical components and software tools; hold our own in aeronautics and make headway in biotechnology, in the gene-mapping of complex organisms, in the neurosciences and in biotechnology's industrial and agro-industrial applications.

The signs are that in innovation Britain is now falling behind. In 1975 Britain secured 4% of the US patents granted to innovators in the US and all over the world. By 1985 the figure had fallen to only 3%. Over the same period, as Britain fell behind, France held its own and not only Japan but Germany did better.

This diminishing contribution to the international pool of new ideas reflects what has happened to British science in general and British scientific manpower in particular. Throughout the Thatcher years the brain drain of top scientists and engineers from Britain has increased, with Britain now losing more scientists to posts across the Atlantic than all other European countries put together. The rate of this emigration

(18 per million population in 1984) was eight times that of Italy and France, five times that of Germany and nearly twice that of Ireland. In 1978, 697 UK scientists were given permanent residence in the USA. By 1985 the figure had risen to 852 and it is still going up. Britain, says Sir David Phillips, the government's own adviser, is losing out as scientific talent emigrates *en masse*. 'We are particularly well endowed with such bright young people in this country and their loss is the saddest and most deplorable result of the philosophy of the present time.'

The view from the other side was reported in the *New York Times* on 22 November 1988: 'The British brain drain began early in the decade but has become a haemorrhage in the last five years, and many of the emigrants blame Prime Minister Margaret Thatcher's government for the exodus ... They are part of a migration that may be the largest single influx into this country from a single source since Jewish professors were forced to leave Germany and Austria in the 1930s.'

It is, however, the quality of the outward flow that gives greatest cause for concern. In the Eighties, far more of our more eminent scientists have moved abroad than ever before. 23% of the Fellows of the Royal Society now live overseas. A 1986 study found that the numbers living permanently outside the UK had risen from 161 in 1979 to 240 at the time of the survey. Between 1979 and 1986 the proportion living in America rose from 6% to 8%

This irreparable loss of national resources has little to do with taxation, for the brain drain has actually intensified since top rate taxes fell. According to Dr Brian Griffiths of Southampton University, it has everything to do with the funding of research and the facilities available for it. As the then Minister for Higher Education admitted in April 1987, 'Young scientists leaving for America are refugees not from the Treasury but from the cumulative effects on British science of educational, industrial, fiscal and cultural failings'.

Perhaps the House of Commons Select Committee on Science and Technology was right to remark that 'many would rather work in the United Kingdom but there were not the facilities there'. And our competitors are taking advantage of this. As Britain downgrades its involvement in European Space Agency projects German firms have been attempting to attract some 400 space engineers specialising in software. Scientists raised and trained here will contribute to the German ESA effort.

In 1987, in one of her familiar, highly publicised initiatives, Mrs Thatcher took control of science policy. In the early 1980s, when scientists had complained about our growing technological backwardness, Mrs Thatcher had said there was no need for a Science Minister. Now, by agreeing to chair the Advisory Committee on Science and Technology, the Prime Minister has put herself at the head of science policy.

Little improvement has resulted. 'The morale of the scientific community has fallen to its lowest point this century,' reported the Royal Society's President, Sir George Porter. 'Our science base is eroding to the point where research-based companies have to recruit scientists from abroad,' claimed Mr John Banham of the CBI on 6 September 1988. In the field of research itself this view is even more widely held. The Chairman of the Advisory Board for the Research Councils, Sir David Philips, said in 1988 that decisions by the government were 'progressively leading to an unstable situation'. They were 'insufficient to avert a reduction in the volume of scientific activity or to allow for the necessary reshaping of the science base'. Philips concludes that 'we remain precariously at the divide and are beginning to slip in the wrong direction'.

Others have been more despondent. On 22 February 1988 the head of physiology at Oxford, Professor Colin Blakemore, stated that 'in my gloomiest moments I think we have lost the future'. And the head of Marck's UK neuroscience labs puts it even more strongly: 'We are committing national suicide.'

Scientists engaged in 'pure research' brought us the unravelling of DNA and thus opened the way for the biotechnology breakthroughs that followed. Crystallography, penicillin and numerous other practical achievements of science all started out as 'pure research'. Research efforts matter to us nationally not only in terms of prestige but in the sterner business of international trade.

Our science-based trade once earned us a surplus of £3 billion a year. Now we are in deficit to the tune of £6 billion. This year the government announced an extra £300 million available for British science, but on closer examination, as Dr Jeremy Bray has demonstrated, little of that turns out to be new money.

Added to that is the neglect of science in schools, the shortage of science teachers and the lack of encouragement for maths and science courses in our universities. As the Board stated in a May 1988 document, Britain's share of world scientific output has been declining because 'UK output has remained fairly constant at a time when the world total has increased significantly . . . Some countries, notably the USA, France and West Germany, have increased scientific output and thus maintained their world share while Japan has dramatically improved its low share.'

By international standards Britain has a very low number of scientists and engineers working in research and development. We employ only 34 for every 10,000 in the total labour force, while France has 41, Germany 62 and America 65. And the government's own contribution to the research and development effort has declined substantially. In 1978 there were 72,000 scientists working in research and development under the government. In 1986 there were only 45,000,due partly to the removal of the UK Atomic Energy Authority from government. But the private sector has not made up the shortfall. In 1975 there were 190,000 at work on research and development in the private sector. Against all international trends this figure had fallen to 188,000 in 1986.

Private sector research and development comprises, as Lord Young has admitted, 'a smaller proportion of our GDP and is growing more slowly than in most major countries'. *But the government's response to this has been to cut the public contribution as well. Even when market forces fail the government refuses to step in.* Faced with the evidence of private sector failure the government's response given in a Common Market document on research policies stated that they did not accept the need for greater public expenditure and argued that more effective management was all that was necessary. 'In general the government believes that R & D in Britain is driven too much by expenditure in the public sector.' It seems they would prefer to see the private sector doing research and development inefficiently than to sponsor public sector science to do it well.

Despite the technological challenges, the pressure of international competition and the opportunities offered by North Sea oil, the government's own expenditure on research and development has actually fallen. At constant 1981 prices, it fell from £1.1 billion in

1978 to £1.05 billion in 1986, the latest year for which figures are available.

In particular, the government's contribution to research and development in industry has fallen. In the Seventies it normally exceeded 30%. Now it is only 23%, but as the government share has fallen there is no evidence of any substantial compensatory increase in funding by the private sector.

The Conservatives' claim is that all 'near-market' research initiatives should be 'the subject of commercial judgement and therefore should be the responsibility of industry'. As they reported to the EEC, 'the balance of existing policies should be changed in order to move away from near-market R & D'. The upshot of this review was the end of the general scheme for providing innovation grant assistance to individual companies. The Microelectronics Industry Support Programme, the Support for Software Products and the Fibreoptics and Optoelectronic Scheme were all severely cut back or phased out, and the government refused to provide follow-up backing for the Alvey programme on information technology.

The tragedy for Britain is that public sector support has been withdrawn without any assurance that the private sector can do the job. The impact on the overall research and development budget has been enormous, as international comparisons confirm. According to the Department of Trade and Industry's figures, Britain spent £6 billion on civil research and development in 1985, when France spent £7 billion and West Germany £11 billion. The latest comparative figures for research and development spending as a percentage of GDP show Britain at only 1.7%, France at 1.8%, the USA at 1.9%, Japan at more than 2% and Germany at 2.5%. In addition, the Netherlands, Sweden and Switzerland all spend more of their national income on research and development than we do.

Perhaps more significantly, while all other countries have been spending more and more on research and development throughout the Eighties, Britain is spending less. The extent to which research investment has fallen behind can be seen from figures calculated from our competitors' investment performance over the last ten years. If, over the last ten years, we had spent as much as France on civil research and development we would have spent £5 billion more; if as much as Germany, £8 billion more; if as much as Sweden, £7.2 billion more. As the *British Medical Journal* has concluded, 'as a percentage of GDP Britain already spends less than all other countries belonging to the OECD, and is spending less as other countries spend more'.

Under Labour in the Seventies research and development in manufacturing industry and expenditure in areas such as electronics grew far more quickly than it has done more recently under the Conservatives. Nowadays it is in the newest areas of industrial activity that we are falling behind most quickly. In information technology, as the House of Commons Select Committee reported, Japan is specialising in fifth generation computers and artificial intelligence techniques. But when the Bide Committee recommended an extension of the Alvey programme, to exploit information technology research and technology transfer, with total funding of £425 million, the government refused. As the Japanese move ahead, the UK's information technology R & D programme consists only of a contribution to the EEC Esprit 2 programme and a £74 million project with SERC and the DTI.

Other countries do it better and take the challenges of the future more seriously. France has designated 'technological poles' in its various regions, for example biotechnology and fine chemicals in Alsace and food, biological and medical engineering in Burgundy. Germany has financed innovation and technology centres, with a view to creating 80 or so. They will concentrate on new, technology-based firms and will maintain a regional dimension but, in their small scale, contrast with the 'technopole' schemes in France and the science parks approach in the UK. Throughout Europe there are far wider fiscal and financial incentives than exist in Britain. In France there is a tax credit equivalent to 25% of increased research costs from one year to the next. Direct financial assistance for specialist technologies, assistance that includes both grants and loans and risk-sharing investments, is even more widespread. Spain offers non-returnable loans, public research facilities, subsidies and capital risk credits. Britain, by contrast, does not provide grants for capital assets and equipment and has cut back on loans.

Outside Europe other countries are moving ahead in research. In Japan applied and development research has always dominated the overall research budget, with basic research taking only 10–15%. Even this is now being questioned: a recent report from the Japanese Science and Technology Administration has called for more public funding for basic research and for post-doctoral research work, drawing attention to the lack of large-scale research facilities and databases and the fact that engineers in Japan outnumber science graduates.

In Taiwan priority has been given to high technology sectors, such as telecommunications, integrated information technology and biotechnology. More than 1% of GDP is allocated to R & D with 14 researchers per 10,000 of population. Even Brazil and India are spending 1% and 0.6% of GDP on R & D respectively, and Israel, Hong Kong, Singapore and Argentina are beginning to catch up.

Britain, formerly a major force in world pharmaceuticals, is now falling behind in this too. Japan manufactures 22% of all new drugs while in the Sixties and Seventies it did only half as well. Despite our traditional involvement in the industry our share has dropped to around 5%. A report prepared by the Economic Advisory Group found that 'the UK is losing strength in those aspects of pure science which are of direct relevance to the pharmaceutical industry . . . There is a feeling that Britain has lost something of its edge . . . One major US company commented that it could not recruit enough researchers of the right calibre for its British centre. The decision to locate in Britain had not been questioned when it was taken five years ago. Now it would be.'

Medical research has deteriorated too. The Academic Medicine Group, representing leading figures in medical education, states that 'academic medicine has suffered severely in the past decade . . . We have to say that it can no longer be assumed that standards of training and research can be maintained at the levels which we have known hitherto' (*Financial Times*, 29 February 1988). Health and safety is one specific area in which the government has admitted to poorer research performance 'because of the constraints on finance and staff to monitor contracts'.

Despite being one of the more aggressively market-oriented of the privatised companies, British Aerospace have, in a recent report, recognised that even 'the efficient market cannot respond in a timely manner and it becomes necessary for both industry and government to make judgements based on a strategic view', and added that 'while industries base judgements on the potential value of a new technology to their profitability, only government is in a position to act in areas where the technology will be of major economic benefit for the nation

47

as a whole ...'. Their conclusion is that there is 'an important place for government as an active participant in the actual generation, finance and performance of research and development. Given the importance of these considerations it makes no sense to talk of a "no policy" R & D stance by government.'

The private sector cannot do the job on its own. In no other developed nation is it even being asked to try. The impact on our international competitiveness is already evident. As a former head of the Alvey directorate put it, 'where projects required significant investment by industry to pull them through the market place ... we are showing real weakness'.

By its neglect of science and innovation, of research and development, the Thatcher government has shown time and time again that it knows the price of everything and the value of nothing. The longer term consequences for our nation can only be guessed at, but in the words of Albert Einstein, writing in 1936, 'intellectual decline brought on by shallow materialism is a far greater menace to the survival of a society than numerous external foes who threaten its existence with violence'.

4

Education and Training: The Betrayal of a Generation

'Under this government we have changed the debate on education away
from the perennial arguments on organisation to the important subjects
of educational standards and parental influence.'

Mrs Thatcher, 1984

'A man must choose . . . between paying for his children's education
and accepting whatever the state provides.'

Mrs Thatcher, 1977

One astonishing fact stands out above all the others in Britain's
education and training record over the Thatcher years: after these
ten years there are now fewer students at college and university in
Britain than there are in South Korea. In the early 1980s Korea
moved ahead of Britain in the international higher education league
table. By the end of the 1980s it will be the turn of Taiwan.

Fifteen years ago Korea had only one quarter of a million students in
higher and vocational education. Britain had three quarters of a million.
Now Britain has just under 1,000,000 and Korea has 1,250,000.
More than 30% of Korea's young adults are in tertiary education,
whereas only 22% of ours are. And when the Education Secretary
declared in February 1989 that he foresaw 'a massive expansion in
higher education' he singularly failed to produce or even promise the
resources that would make it possible. Our education and training
will continue to fall back. We have long since failed to match West
Germany and recently fallen behind Korea. We aspire now to keep
up not with the Japanese, but with the Taiwanese.

Investment in education promotes not only economic growth but
social justice too. Through education individuals realise their potential

49

and develop their talents to the full. In the Eighties, the debate should have been about how best to provide education at any time, at any level of study and at any age. The goal should have been permanent, recurrent and lifelong education, since a modern economy will flourish only by mobilising the talents of the majority for the challenge of permanent innovation.

The goal of equal opportunities should have been realised by proper and adequate educational provisions, but it is clear now that educational reform, Tory-style, is preoccupied with selection for the benefit of the few and has nothing to do with expanding opportunities available to the many. Tory emphasis has been on yet more structural reorganisation: on city technology colleges, on opt-out schools, on assisted places, on creating markets in education, on a pecking-order of schools which will yield third, fourth and fifth divisions in education, effectively on the creation of a market in children and their future.

Government ministers are more willing to provide public subsidies for new tiers of privilege in education than they are to attend to pressing problems in existing schools in the public system, half of which are considered by Her Majesty's Inspectors to be in urgent need of physical improvement. While privilege is being created, general provisions are crumbling. Talents of individual and national value are being wasted as a result of educational policies that are both divisive and regressive.

In Mrs Thatcher's view the crucial requirement for wealth creation is not a broadly educated workforce of the many but the visionary entrepreneurship of the few: an individual combination of energy, initiative and drive for selling or trading that thrives in a kind of caricature economy more like the rag trade than the real thing. It is a view that has failed the nation, because the British economy of the future, if it is going to be competitive, will depend on the diffusion of the majority of the skills now enjoyed only by the minority. Without a well-trained workforce Britain will find it increasingly difficult to match the productivity and income growth of other countries.

According to a Bow Group study, businessmen are now more worried about the consequences for the economy of educational decline than they are about the traditional Tory bogey, the power of the unions. The CBI appreciate the problem even if the government does not, stating in their *Business Manifesto* that young people 'in the bottom 40% of the ability range receive much less benefit from 11 years of education than their counterparts in countries such as Germany . . . The aim should be to have the same proportion of young people in this country completing higher education as there are in countries such as Japan and the US.'

Yet during the 1980s Britain had a chance to make the leap into the advanced education of the future but short-sighted politicians failed us. Britain, concludes one study by Finegold and Soskice, is 'trapped in a low skills equilibrium in which the majority of enterprises, staffed by poorly trained managers and workers, produce low quality goods and services. The term equilibrium is used to connote a self-reinforcing network of societal and state institutions which interact to stifle the demand for improvements in skill levels.'

The facts which put British education in perspective make grim reading. Today no European country except Greece has such a small proportion of its teenagers staying on at school as Britain. None sees so few go on to higher and further education. America and the Pacific-rim countries have 80–90% of the age group staying on at school beyond 16. In Japan the figure is 95%. We have no more than 80%, either in full-time education or in highly structured apprenticeships. And no European country has such a large proportion of its workforce without any qualifications at all. 40% have no GCE O-level and for well over half the highest qualification achieved is that of GCE O-level.

The net result is that at the end of the 1980s Britain has higher proportions of untrained workers than has any of our international rivals. As Sanderson shows in the *Oxford Review of Economic Policy*, 60% of German manufacturing workers had at least intermediate qualifications while less than 30% were similarly qualified in the UK. As Lord Young had to admit, 'the training and skills of our managers and other employees are low compared with our principal competitors'.

Our current skill shortages are an obvious result, and there are many examples. The Channel Tunnel is now being built using engineers from Egypt and Hong Kong. British firms recruit graduates abroad and British firms take apprentices abroad for proper training because they cannot obtain it here. Investment in skills is vital to our economic future but in every area of skill training Britain is lagging behind. As Mr Roger Dawe, the Tory-appointed head of the new Government

Training Agency, confessed, 'at every level we are towards the bottom of the training league table, whether in education, youth training, higher level skills training or management training'.

Our present workforce therefore boasts a daunting majority of the unskilled and the low-skilled. Where skills exist they are commonly inadequate. The most recent studies suggest that much of our productivity failure has arisen from inadequate education and training. One writer, comparing Germany and the UK, concluded that 'the most important overall implication of the study is that the lack of technical expertise and training ... is the stumbling block'. There have been many other warnings, all ignored by the government. Other recent research corroborated the overall picture of technological advance blocked and blighted by the inadequate education of entrants to industry and a subsequent failure in industry to address the chronic and widespread problems of education and training.

In 1988 the CBI completed an Anglo-German report entitled *Tales of Two Companies*. Its conclusion was that 'given the UK firm's poorer productivity record we infer that this must be due in large measure to the lower quality of the workforce ... The UK must persist in its efforts to improve the basic education of its people, for as we have seen it is this factor above all else that accounts for the difference in industrial performance between itself and its major competitor.'

Neglect of basic education starts in the schools, indeed in nursery schools and in the lack of them. Despite a promise from the former Education Minister, now Prime Minister, of nursery education for all, very few in Britain today enjoy access to it. The general provision is low, and worse under Tory education authorities, which offer nursery education on only half the scale of their Labour-controlled neighbours.

The neglect of all education has been a feature of the Thatcher years: we now spend less of our national income on education and science than we did in 1979, its share having fallen from 4.5% to 3.9%. Between 1979 and 1988 the amount central government spends on schools was cut by 17% or £790 million. Capital spending on schools has been cut by £190 million or 32% since 1979. £3.13 billion is now needed to bring school buildings up to standard. Between 1990 and 1992 the real value of local authority current spending on schools and further education is to be held level. Such are the constraints imposed by central authority and funding that in many areas the education system has survived only because local authorities have been prepared to ignore government plans.

Education in general matters and education in computers is vital to our industrial future, yet the latest government allocation of funds specifically for information technology amounted to only £10 million for all the nation's schools. And if the most modern computer facilities are not adequately provided in our schools neither are books and other basic materials. Private schools spend an average of £56 per pupil per year on equipment. In the public sector only £38 is spent in secondary schools and £25 in primaries. And in Britain total secondary school spending per pupil is around 7% lower than in America and 12% lower than in France.

In the subjects of maths, science and languages, teacher shortages are such that the Chief Inspector of Schools has reported that any reforms proposed by the government are threatened. In some schools between a quarter and a third of teachers leave each year and teacher shortages, bad enough now, will become worse when in a few years the number of potential entrants begins to decline. Even on the government's own optimistic estimates, by 1995 Britain will be short of 1,000 maths teachers, 1,500 chemistry teachers, 2,500 language teachers and 6,000 technology teachers.

The Joint Council of Languages Associations has warned that 'a shortage of language teachers is endangering government preparations for the single European market in 1992'. Lord Young is less concerned. In his view, 'the knowledge of languages is less important than having a single European market'. The government short-term response to the teacher shortage is to minimise its importance. Its longer-term plan is to dilute standards by recruiting personnel as teachers who have no qualifications.

The end result of all this neglect is that British school leavers are not only younger but a lot less well qualified than those of our major competitors. 53% leave at 16, the earliest possible opportunity. If Britain had the same staying-on rate as the USA, Japan or Germany one million more would be in further education. As things are, they leave, and 40% of them leave with no O-level qualifications at all.

And after school? In Germany 600,000 young people a year enter training and follow a three-year programme that leads to a nationally recognised qualification. Each year Germany provides training and qualifications for between two and three times our numbers of fitters, electricians and building craftsmen. Even young shop workers receive organised and recognised training.

Here in the UK we do these things differently, if indeed we do them at all. The National Council for Vocational Qualifications has not yet established a nationally agreed set of vocational qualifications. Its proposals have already been denounced by an expert as leading to the creation of 'a certificated semi-literate underclass, a section of the workforce inhibited in job flexibility and in the possibility of progression'.

While future possibilities are unconvincing current arrangements are not working. Two-thirds of 16 and 17-year-old school leavers now enter YTS but already the scheme has proved a failure in generating a qualified workforce among the young. Despite the introduction of a one-year YTS in 1983 and a two-year version in 1986 the number of young people obtaining basic craft qualifications has actually fallen. In 1975, for example, 15,600 passed City and Guilds Course 200 at Part 1 level. In 1985 only 8,000 did. In 1975, 22,000 obtained Engineering Training Board Basic Training Certification but in 1988 only 8,000.

As one report comparing youth training in France, Germany and Britain concluded, 'in France two-thirds of shop floor workers held a CAP qualification or higher. In the corresponding British firms we visited less than one in six had the nearest equivalent qualification. And that is scarcely likely to improve in the near future since between 1986 and 1988 more than 76% of YTS trainees received no qualifications and 15% received only one. The two-year training period offers insufficient time to develop the higher skills needed by many occupations. In Germany the majority of manual and non-manual apprentice programmes last three years. In the words of an Essex study, YTS has merely 'encouraged much over-expanded, low-cost low-skill training whose trainees compete with part-time adults for minimal skill jobs'.

It is not easy to imagine the French or German governments boasting about cuts made in investment for trainees, but last year the British government announced that it had achieved a 10% cut in gross cost per trainee since 1985 and hoped for a further 6% cut by 1991. The cash value of investment in 1985 was £237 per trainee each month but has fallen now to £206.

Given the current state of school education and vocational education it might be expected that British firms would be making special efforts in the form of training for personnel in work. The facts, however, are not encouraging. British employers claim to have spent £18 billion on training in 1986–87. Half their employees received training of some sort in that year, on average 14 days. Much of that, around 40%, was focused on employees under 25 years old. Only a fraction of all workers received training both on and off the job, the vast majority receiving only less expensive on-job training. This reflects what the MSC and NEDO have called 'complacency' in the wake of training cut-backs made during the recession of the early 1980s.

Other countries simply do it better. They take training seriously and spend money on it. In the early Eighties German employers were spending about three times as much on training as their British counterparts. Overall, British firms are estimated to spend 0.15% of their turnover on training. In Japan, Germany and France a more typical figure would be between 1% and 2%.

At the level of graduate employment the picture is equally gloomy. In 1960 both Britain and Japan had around 200,000 graduate engineers. Now Japan has a million more than we have, and between 100,000 and 150,000 graduating every year. The Engineering Council looked at the two nations in detail in 1988 and found that Japanese output of engineering graduates per head of population is about two-and-a-half times that of Britain.

Nor do the qualifications of British managers inspire much confidence for our technological future. Only 24% of them, according to Professor Charles Handy, have even City and Guilds, A-levels or equivalent qualifications. The remaining 76% do not, and many of them left school at the minimum age. In Japan and America, where higher education is less specialised, 85% of senior executives have degrees, compared to only 25% in Britain. The 1985 Labour Force Survey revealed that 20% of British managers have no qualifications whatsoever and only 12% of them have a first degree or more advanced qualification.

Mr Channon, a Trade Minister in 1986, had to admit that seven out of every ten managers in British industry get no training at all for their management role at any time during their career and only 5% can boast any formal training in the course of a year. Proportionately we have fewer graduate managers than the USA, Germany, France and Japan, and the really bad news is that we struggle on with less than half the graduate management complement of France, the next worst off in that list of our competitors. In America every year 60,000 candidates gain Master of Business Administration degrees, in Britain only 1,500. This is hardly surprising when it is considered that more than half the companies in the UK make absolutely no provision for the training of senior personnel.

Smallest companies do least, with three-quarters of companies with less than 50 staff doing nothing at all. But even among the largest employers, those with 1,000 or more, only 20% provide senior management training. Truly this is a cultural problem, in which low-skill management is the cultural norm. The battle is one against entrenched amateurism.

From top to bottom British industry is beset by difficulties and shortcomings in training and education. Something has to be done. The government considers all aspects and decides, astonishingly, to do even less. The training gap, it has decreed, will best be closed by handing all responsibility for it over to the very people who have failed so conspicuously in the past. What hope now of a solution from the agents and forces that created the problem? If the free market were capable of resolving the training and education deficits in British industry they simply would not have arisen.

Even Mr Baker's modest proposal for tax relief for training, something he has told the Chancellor other countries seem to be able to afford, has been turned down. Mr Lawson was unimpressed by his assertion that 'the UK would appear to be less generous than most at a time when maximum encouragement is needed if there is to be a new approach to adult training'.

The White Paper on training makes three proposals, each one dependent upon giving employers 'prime responsibility': to secure for every young person vocational training; to encourage provision of training accessible to adults; and to ensure that all concerned with training have access to the information they need to make decisions about training. 'Prime responsibility' is to rest with employers, who will dominate the National Training Task Force and the 100 Training and Enterprise Councils, and who in turn will subcontract activities to training providers in market-based training systems.

There are few believers and many doubters. According to the Scottish section of the British Institute of Management, 'The central premise on which the proposals are based is that much greater involvement will be forthcoming if private business is given ownership of the enterprise. We know of no evidence to support such an assumption.' The Scottish Council admits that 'it may be difficult to attract businessmen of the quality and numbers required to take up quasi-executive positions in the new, very large structure'. And there are, of course, no plans to increase resources. Spending by the Training Agency will undergo a real fall, by 4% each year until 1992.

Current problems are vast and future goals clear. There is nothing in the government's main responses so far — the discredited YTS and the elaborate, unfunded and unbelievable new scheme — that inspires the least confidence. In ten years nothing has been achieved even in the comparatively modest task of moulding a system of education and training to fit our workforce for the challenges of today.

Worse still, Britain is now moving backwards, not just failing to improve its education system, but fragmenting it, creating new divisions and new anomalies of funding by such means as opt-out schools, privately funded colleges and universities and student loans. City Technology Colleges are a case in point: originally to be funded entirely by the private sector, they are now the recipients of generous government subsidies. A cost-free option becomes costly and the education budget is finite, so support for state schools is cut back and students are invited to pay their way with loans.

In 1979 there was no great demand for private education. Now, with the state sector deteriorating under the constant pressure of inadequate funding, more parents are seeking an alternative where none should ever have been necessary. Private sector fees are high, at least £3,000 a year now and likely to rise substantially over the next decade, and assisted place schemes cover only a small minority, with less than 5,000 for England and Wales in 1988. In the years ahead entry into private schools is likely to remain confined to the higher income groups. Throughout the Eighties the real education issue for Britain — that of improving the quality of education for the many — has been obscured.

The far greater challenges of the immediate future have remained unaddressed. Tomorrow's workforce needs more than education and training to current international standards. It must be equipped for a continuously evolving high-technology working environment, for the perpetual innovation required to keep abreast of an increasingly competitive market for high quality goods and services. Demographic change and the falling numbers of teenagers offer a chance to improve quality in education and training of school leavers. Higher education, currently under attack, must be developed to provide more places both in science and technology and in management studies. If we do nothing (or — the current Tory alternative — nothing that works) then we are doomed to remain trapped in the stagnation of the low-skill equilibrium and sink slowly down that ever more alarming international league table.

Only the government believes that government intervention can be avoided. Sir Francis Toombs, chairman of the Engineering Council and an adviser to the Prime Minister, puts the point accurately when he says that 'normal market forces will not work to make up the severe shortfall and provide the skills base needed by modern industry and commerce'.

Most commentators and participants in industry now recognise that it would be wrong if the very companies who have failed to deliver in the past should take responsibility for training in the future. Supply side socialism acknowledges that very few companies indeed are self-sufficient in training and that the government role in support of productive training can and should be a large one.

A few months ago a Tory-dominated select committee warned that in the fast-expanding sector of information technology there is a manpower crisis in both quality and quantity. In the field of computer science alone the CBI believes that a failure to take training seriously 'could leave Britain dangerously exposed compared with its international rivals'.

The free market has failed to solve the problems and the international competition continues to improve. Public investment is required and is long overdue. A rational approach to our national self-interest now dictates a strong government-led and funded expansion of education and training directed at increasing our national competitiveness. Despite ten years of Tory neglect there may yet be time.

5

Rundown Britain

To make a few individuals rich the government has been prepared to make all our communities poor. It has been willing to tolerate rising incomes for some side by side with rising discomfort, inconvenience and squalor for others. This encouragement of private affluence at the price of public squalor is characteristic and intentional. For many citizens and most visitors to the UK the results are as obvious as they are unwelcome: a visible and continually frustrating legacy of the Thatcher years.

Britain in the late Eighties has the look of a rundown nation, but it is not simply a matter of appearances. 40% of our trunk roads have an expected life of less than ten years, 25% of our local roads less than five. One sewage pipe in six is more than a hundred years old. One third of our water supply is lost through leakage from old and poorly maintained pipelines. Half of the beds used by the National Health Service are in accommodation built before 1914. Three-quarters of its ward blocks are hand-me-downs from the days of charity, voluntary and municipal hospitals.

A million children are being taught in classrooms built before 1914 and many of these classrooms are now structurally unstable. According to the Audit Commission there is a maintenance timebomb, it is only a matter of time 'before it becomes necessary to close schools for safety reasons'. After a broader review the CBI has concluded that 'the deterioration in the conditions of Britain's roads and sewerage systems, schools and public housing is continuing, piling up bills for the future which will be more expensive with every year's delay'.

Tourists coming to the Britain described by the British Tourist Authority are poorly prepared for the realities they encounter. In comparison with what they have seen elsewhere our public services

59

are underfunded and over-extended. The civic pride that maintains services and appearances in cities like Zurich and Marseilles is backed by funding and effective organisation. In most of Britain's major cities, civic apologies are more in order. But cities devoutly wishing to look better and run better are prevented from doing so by the doctrinaire and penny-pinching diktats of central government.

A great civic heritage is decaying. The public buildings, parks, and railways of which we were once proud are declining into crumbling squalor in a manner that would have greatly puzzled the Victorians who built them. For the Tories of today, public institutions are symbolic of decadence, of the incompleteness of the desired dominance of the private sector. Their diminution, by assault or neglect, is an important agenda item for a government which, as one academic has written, 'takes the attrition of the public world as the expression of the people's preferences' and is well on its way to creating 'an England whose households ape California and whose public domain struggles to avoid the damnation of the South Bronx'. Private affluence, he concludes, will 'lose all its savour amidst public squalor . . . A growing army of the British people feel the irrationality of spending more and more of their private income to purchase exemption from the environmental decay.'

In their own reports to the European Commission, government ministers have been honest enough to admit the sheer scale of the problem: the decaying and deteriorating buildings, services and amenities of our cities and regions. In their own words, south Yorkshire had an 'obsolescent and degrading physical environment' with 'colliery spoil heaps and waste lagoons' and an 'ageing and unsound infrastructure. In the West Midlands 'industrial dereliction is widespread', and there is a 'stark legacy of decayed infrastructure, poor physical and environmental conditions and low standards of social and neighbourhood facilities'. And as the report states, 'much of the intra-regional public transport system is in need of renewal and improvement'.

Yet there is no convincing economic case for the curb on public investment. If it is good for the private sector to invest in the gas industry or in buses it is surely good for the public sector to invest in its railways, hospitals and schools. Public investments are capable of improvement, and widely in need of it, and are certainly not immune from obsolescence or decay. For too long a myth has been propagated and widely accepted: that it is somehow a better use of resources for the private sector to invest in, say, casinos or amusement arcades than for the public sector to invest in our schools, our roads, our railways and in our infrastructure generally.

Such investment is long overdue and its results will be greatly welcomed if and when it can be effected. Meanwhile, amid the rising tide of public squalor which only major public investment will reverse, Mrs Thatcher has taken unto herself a very special cause, that of litter. Her approach has been entirely typical, combining the simplistic, the exhortatory and the short-sighted meanness of 'angry ratepayer, W.1'. In Mrs Thatcher's view the problem can more or less be solved by nagging the nation often enough. The UK 2000 campaign is largely a propaganda exercise, and its inception has not prevented the loss of 10,000 of Britain's 60,000 street orderlies.

Yet, as Michael Ignatieff has written, 'It would not occur to Mrs Thatcher that litter is a symptom of decay in a public environment starved of expenditure and imagination. Clean streets depend on the interrelationship between private virtue and public institutions, between people who care enough to struggle against the defacement of public places and the public officials who will back up their commitment with investment.'

Nowhere is the failure to invest and to plan more obvious than in our overcrowded , underfinanced, underplanned, undermaintained and sometimes dangerous transport system. Within the last 12 months there have been unprecedented incidences of delay, congestion and, in the cases of King's Cross, Clapham and Purley, horrific loss of life. And in the year before there was the disaster at Zeebrugge.

Today our roads and railways are congested, our airports and airways uncomfortably and sometimes dangerously crowded, road and rail maintenance in disarray and safety now a major issue in the public mind. Yet for the government the real issue in transport is not quality of service or safety but the puzzling obsession with privatisation. 1990 will begin with rail privatisation threatening rural train services and a government study addressing the feasibility of executive fast lanes — and privatisation — for our roads.

After the airlines, airports, seaports, ferry services, coaches and buses, the government's central objective in transport is more privatisation. Their first aim is to increase efficiency and reduce real unit costs . . .

by policies to increase competition and to decrease the role of the public sector. Standards of service, accessibility and accountability, even considerations of safety take priority far below that single overriding imperative. Their 1987 manifesto does not even mention safety or quality of service as objectives of transport policy.

Almost everyone except government ministers recognises there is a need for an integrated transport system, and such a system would be a more efficient use of national resources. Yet since the government abandoned the idea of coordinated transport planning the transport system has become increasingly chaotic. In London 25 separate programmes and investment schemes are being run by 33 London boroughs and ten other agencies — all without proper coordination. As the *Sunday Times* recently remarked, 'Other countries take this in their stride, seeing the government's job as providing the best system to support the general economy and where necessary using taxpayers' money to oil the wheels. Britain resists any suggestion of planning and watches the traffic jams grow.'

Changes in ownership, as Dr Stuart Cole of the North London Business School argues, cannot solve the problems of congestion in the absence of a coordinated policy. 'We are living in an *Alice in Wonderland* world at the moment because the wisdom which has been accepted for twenty-five years or more has been progressively undermined over the last five years and is being turned on its head.' And as the Royal Town Planning Institute has said in a recent letter to Mr Channon, the Transport Minister, 'We are being increasingly asked to accept the principle of the marketplace — a market which pays no direct regard to the costs of accidents and policing, to pollution and other forms of environmental damage, or to delays and reductions in travel opportunities experienced by others.' As the Institute's President concluded, 'Our towns and cities are just going to die if we do not take these issues seriously'.

Transport should be safe, reliable, convenient and as cheap as possible and such transport serves national as well as individual goals. Our competitor nations recognise this and invest accordingly. In the most recent comparisons Britain does very badly indeed, spending only 0.6% of the national income on inland transport, on which Germany spends almost twice as much at 1.1%. At 0.9%, the European average is significantly higher than our figure. Ten years ago Britain's transport investment as a proportion of national income was greater than Italy's. Now we have fallen behind. Even Spain spends a greater share than we do on transport.

Most other European countries not only spend on transport but plan as well. Across Europe there is a blueprint for high-speed rail and the upgrading of existing track. All this enjoys a proper subsidy, but under the Conservatives the real value of rail investment has fallen well behind that of our European competitors. In 1984, the last year in which comparable figures are available, Britain had invested only £1 for every £2 invested n France, for every £2.5 invested in Italy and for every £5 invested in Germany.

Yet where investment has occurred in the rail system of Britain it has paid off. When, for example, the Bedford to St Pancras and Moorgate line was modernised and electrified there was a 40% increase in traffic. As the Monopolies Commission commented, 'the key to this was the concurrent improvement of a number of aspects of service quality'. A similar package of rail improvements in the Cardiff area brought a 55% increase in passenger traffic and a 40% increase in revenue.

As the existing transport system deteriorates and the challenge of the Channel Tunnel draws nearer the need for investment is greater than ever, but constraints on the amounts the railways may borrow to invest have tightened, and government grants for the railways have fallen steadily over the last ten years. In 1979 they amounted to £831 million, and they fell successively to £500 million in 1988–9.

In France investment has been higher and public financial support greater. SNCF tracks allow safe speeds of up to 145 mph, while many BR tracks are limited to 60 mph use at peak periods. The TGV line has allowed passenger travel to increase by six million a year since it was opened in 1982 and two million of these are passengers new to rail travel. France is also introducing a computerised system for the automated control of single wagon deliveries and a highly integrated computerised signal network. A high-speed European line linking the German, French and Italian high-speed systems is planned. Switzerland and Denmark are both undertaking major upgrading of their rail systems.

The whole of Europe, with the exception of Britain, seems to be committed to an efficient and properly funded rail system. Here in Britain public financial support for rail investment has fallen by 40%, with a further 40% cut planned for 1990–91, severely limiting BR's ability to prepare for the future. In addition, the government, anticipating BR's privatisation, has imposed strict requirements on the returns BR must generate from new investment. These ignore the wider social and economic benefits that stem from rail investment and have been used by the Scottish Office to deny BR the money it needs to build a rail bridge over the Dornoch Firth. No such limits apply to road investment: money will be forthcoming for a Dornoch Firth road bridge.

A comparison between Network Southeast and the Paris rail system is instructive. Despite the fact the NSE is a much larger system, servicing 34% more passenger kilometres, its average annual investment is actually 10% less, with obvious detrimental effects. NSE is overcrowded. Since 1983 the number of railway passenger seats available has fallen by 11% but the number of passenger journeys has dropped by only 1%. In 1986 the average loading on NSE trains was 4.2% above the maximum target loadings for the sector.

The passenger load per train, which averaged 78% in 1982, is now 128%. On intercity and provincial services overcrowding is not systematically monitored but problems are certainly being encountered. The number of passenger complaints received by BR doubled between 1982 and 1985. It would be interesting to know how complaints figures have evolved since, but BR has stopped reporting them. However, claims against BR for consequential damages in connection with delays have more than doubled.

On the London underground the overcrowding, as every user knows, is far worse. Travel has increased from 594 million passenger journeys in 1979 to 798 million in 1988. Over the years this represents a 40% rise in use. The number of railway cars in use has gone up by only 10%. Government support for London Regional Transport's investment, which was £351 million in 1985, immediately after it was brought under government control, was reduced to £256 million in 1988–9 and will be only £253 million in the coming year despite all the improvements, including those relating to safety, which now must be made in the aftermath of the King's Cross inquiry. Much of what has been spent went on the purchase of the Victoria Coach Station, and investment has simply not gone where it was needed.

Parts of the London underground system are now 120 years old.

The escalator on which the King's Cross fire took place was 50 years old. The QC for the King's Cross inquiry argued that the disaster revealed 'an endemic and long-standing underinvestment in the technology which is presently available to operate an underground railway with increasing degrees of safety' (*Financial Times*, 26 June 1988). The 1988 Passengers' Committee report on the underground spoke of 'High levels of cancellations, long delays, potentially dangerous levels of overcrowding ... the lack of working lifts and escalators' and concluded that, 'Never in the life of this committee have more people complained about the service on London underground'.

The underground systems of London and Paris make a worrying contrast. The Paris underground is also an antique, but a decision has been taken to make it reliable, clean and safe. London has taken a different decision, with familiar results, and has a system that is both second best and dangerous. While our European neighbours accept that public transport is vital to the efficient running of a city this government does not. Subsidies in Parisian public transport run at around 80%, those in London at a niggardly 20%. Elsewhere, in Turin, Rome, Amsterdam, Bonn and even Los Angeles public subsidies are far higher, ranging from 50% to 80%. The issue at stake is one of economic efficiency. Bad public transport is costly in many unexpected ways. As the CBI has warned, 'If we are not careful we are going to lose London as a major European commercial centre'.

Good public transport promotes safety as well as commercial life. When the Greater London Council reduced its fares public transport passengers rose by 16%, car journeys went down by 10% and road traffic accident injuries fell by 3,000. Underfunded public transport, however, has its own special dangers. Even the personal safety of passengers on trains has been diminished by the reduction of the numbers of guards. There are now 3,300 fewer than there were in 1979, and muggings on trains, such as those on the Bedford line, have become more frequent. The Clapham train crash inquiry has revealed the pressures on staff and systems brought about by financial constraints.

Even the inspectorate that should enforce transport safety standards has itself been hit by economies. In the annual report of the Chief Inspecting Officer for British Rail it is seen how the Rail Inspectorate was undermanned by more than a third last year. As a result its efforts

65

to monitor in the interests of safety the activities of managements more concerned with economy than safety have been hampered by the same absurd insistence on further economy in a transport system already grossly underfunded. Always from the top comes the cry for cheaper rather than safer.

An identical preference for the claims of economy over those of safety is found at sea. In 1981 Merchant Navy officers with Townsend Thoronson lines threatened strike action over ship manning levels and specifically demanded an officer available to ensure that a single officer would not be expected to supervise two operations simultaneously, one at the bow doors, the other on the bridge. In February 1982 the extra manpower was refused. In 1986, when a ferry capsized and 193 lives were lost, the supervision available was finally demonstrated to be disastrously inadequate. Basic design faults in roll-on roll-off ferries were also identified, but the official inquiry commented damningly 'from top to bottom the body corporate was infected with the disease of sloppiness'.

Safety in the air is also a matter of increasing public concern, with survey reports that two-thirds of passengers are prepared to pay more in order to travel more safely. Alarm continues, with 55 near-misses reported in UK airspace in 1987 and 61 in 1986. Again, undermanning and an excessive regard for short-sighted economy seem to have played their part. At West Drayton, an air traffic control centre responsible for some of the busiest airspace in the world, controller staff is sometimes under strength by as much as 40. And following the privatisation of the British Airports Authority, security at our airports has been shown to be grossly inadequate, with financial responsibility for security a matter for dispute between BAA and the public sector.

On our roads the nostrums of free market capitalism have been applied to bus transport but few would claim that improvement has resulted. Certainly patronage of bus services has gone down. The intended competition is rare, with only 5% of routes actually offering it, and in Merseyside deregulation actually reduced the number of passenger journeys by 20%. Since 1985 subsidies from central government have fallen by more than £100 million. Government grants for new buses, worth £80 million in 1980, have now been phased out. Support for concessionary fares has fallen over the years and the number of people employed has gone down by 40,000 to 166,000 since 1979. After all the fuss and disruption the private sector share is only 13% and in the view of the Public Transport Campaign Group deregulation has brought only chaos, confusion and cuts in services.

The underfunding of public transport has forced more goods and people on to our roads where, as every driver knows, there are chronic problems of overcrowding and delay. The CBI states that the costs of transport congestion are now about £15 billion a year, and argues that our transport system is so poor that when the Channel Tunnel is completed northern France is more likely to benefit than the north of England from the south of England's inevitable overspill. It is now quicker to cycle from Bristol to Poole than it is to travel by lorry. And the CBI also estimates that delays on the M25, which was scarcely opened before it became overcrowded, now mean another £1 billion in extra costs for industry. The Royal Mail says London's traffic jams add £10 million a year to its operating costs, whilst Sainsbury's claim congestion costs them an extra £3.4 million a year.

Local authorities' attempts at improvements in transport systems have been undermined by government cutbacks in the rate support grant. This has forced transport to compete with other local government spending priorities in budgets already stretched to the limit. Transport 2000 has pointed out how a new government announcement will mean further cuts in grants to local authorities for the construction of metro and light railway systems.

Britain, if it is to compete in the Nineties, must plan for an integrated transport system and proper investment in transport. Such a transport policy must encompass improvements in public transport, environmental protection and traffic restraint in urban areas. Proper investment in transport will reduce congestion and help the economy, not only improving the quality of life for many but making us more competitive by supporting economic regeneration and offering improved efficiency to industry.

Yet the government response to every problem in transport is not to admit that investment is needed and planning long overdue, but to press onwards with its programme of privatisation. 1990 will begin with more privatisation measures. British Rail is the likeliest major candidate and rail services will suffer accordingly. One estimate (*Guardian*, 3 November 1988) put the price of rail privatisation as the loss of 1,000 miles of track, mainly rural and branch lines, so that in some regions only the main arteries would remain. Lesser measures, such as the executive fast lanes under discussion, already tried in Spain and regarded there as a failure, would bring problems.

A free market in transport would represent a triumph of doctrine over experience, a sacrifice of the public interest for private profit and a very considerable handicap in our long struggle for national competitiveness. And no less an authority than Sir Colin Buchanan describes it as 'a recipe for total chaos'.

6

Abandoning the Regions

'There was more industrialisation in the North, originally, therefore there now has to be more de-industrialisation. Until 70 years ago the North was always the richest part of the country. The two present growth industries — the City and tourism — are concentrated in the South. I try to encourage people to go North; that is where all the great country houses are because that's where the wealth was. Now some of it is in the South. It's our turn, that's all.'

Lora Young (Quoted in Business, 1987, p. 48)

In Mrs Thatcher's housewife-stateswoman's book of sins there can be few worse than waste, yet the policy of her government towards the regions is characterised by a wastefulness that beggars description. People, communities, towns, whole regions have suffered. Human and material resources have been wasted on a vast scale. The wasteful absurdity of Tory regional policy condemns one part of the country to economic overheating, with skill shortages, congestion, escalating house prices and pressure on the green belt, while others suffer high and persistent unemployment, forced emigration, depopulation and decline.

We have been denied all the advantages of a rational and equitable regional policy for balanced economic development throughout Britain. Such a policy would have helped not only the more hard-pressed regions but would have maximised the benefits of prosperity for the more fortunate, to the advantage of the nation as a whole. But never, even in the Thirties, has the gulf between regions widened so quickly as it has done under the Thatcher government and never has it resulted in so much waste. But one fact stands out, demonstrating beyond doubt the government's failure to achieve balanced economic development. The regions have been growing at almost half the rate of the economies of the South. While the South-West has had average growth of 3.1% a year,

East Anglia 4% a year and, with the South-East included, the southern triangle at just under 3% a year, growth rates in the regions and nations to the North have been anything between 1% and 2%, and have averaged only 1.6%.

Nor is the regional divide likely to narrow in the coming years, as regional grants disappear and public investment continues to fall. Recently the Director General of the CBI predicted how, with new conditions after 1992, things could get very much worse, with the virtual exclusion of new jobs, new industries and new investment north of London. Investment in the infrastructure has been so poor, he suggests, that the northern parts of Great Britain cannot benefit substantially from the internal market: 'On present plans it is all too likely that the growth that 1992 will generate will be enjoyed not in the North-East or South-West but in North-East France . . . Suppliers in Bruges will be better placed than those in Bradford to supply stores in South London.' Such conclusions are similar to those of a confidential Scottish Office study which recognises that the absence of new regional policy measures will leave Scottish industry vulnerable as it faces the challenges of 1992.

Without ever formally adopting a policy of separate development for the two nations over which they now preside, Tory ministers have gone a very long way in that direction. Misguided monetary policies have caused jobs to be lost throughout the whole country, but far from evenly. Since 1979 nearly 1.5 million of the 2 million manufacturing jobs lost have been in regions outside the South. Manufacturing employment has fallen by 29% in the West Midlands, 30% in Wales, 36% in Yorkshire, the North and in Scotland and 38% in the North-West.

It is therefore not surprising that unemployment in the regions has risen faster than the national average. As Table 1 shows, unemployment in Scotland, which was 2% above the national average in 1979, is more than 3% above it in 1988. The same is true of the North, where the excess over average has risen from 3.0% to 3.8%, the North-West, which has gone from 1.2% to 2.5% up, and Northern Ireland, where the gap was 4.2% but is now 8.5%.

And high regional unemployment persists despite high regional emigration. In 1986, for example, there was a net emigration from the North of 6,000 in the key 15–44 age group, with 12,000 from Scotland and 20,000 from the North-West. Jobs have gone and people have gone too from the North and the Midlands, and the gap between North and

South has widened because the North has borne a far higher share of
Britain's industrial closures. One survey found that Tyne and Wear and
Northern Ireland had lost 10% and 15% of their employment
respectively through closures of manufacturing branch plants, while the
figure for communities such as South Hampshire had been only 5%.

Table 1   Relative unemployment performance

Region	Mid-1979		End 1988		Rel. Change
	Rate	Diff.	Rate	Diff.	
South-East	3.0	1.9	4.5	2.7	+0.8
South-West	4.8	0.1	5.4	1.8	+1.7
East Anglia	3.7	1.2	4.1	3.1	+1.9
West Midlands	4.8	0.1	7.5	−0.3	−0.4
East Midlands	4.0	0.9	6.5	0.7	−0.2
Yorkshire Humberside	5.1	−0.2	8.5	−1.3	−1.1
North-West	6.1	−1.2	9.7	−2.5	−1.3
North	7.9	−3.0	11.0	−3.8	−0.8
Wales	6.5	−1.6	9.5	−2.3	−0.7
Scotland	6.9	−2.0	10.5	−3.3	−1.3
Northern Ireland	9.1	−4.2	15.7	−8.5	−4.3
UK	4.9		7.2		

Source: Training Agency Labour Market Quarterly Report

Figures for employment show the expected regional disparities.
Employment figures include the less reliable government figures for
self-employment, but even when these are accepted employment since
1979 has fallen in the North and the Midlands. In Scotland, Wales,
the North and the North-West it is still between 8% and 12% down
on the 1979 levels, and in Northern Ireland it is nearly 7% down on
1979.

Over the past ten years the Tories have at the same time allowed the
regional divide to widen and denied that it exists. In area after area they
have created an industrial desert and called it recovery. Triumphs of
monetarism have been claimed and grim realities denied. And, as a
result, for ten years the regions have been prevented from making their
full contribution to the national economy. And towards the end of those
ten years, as interest rates were raised to curb overheating in the South-
East, the regions suffered even more severely.

Table 2 Regional employment changes in 10 years
employed and self employed
June 1979–June 1988

	% changes in employees	% changes employees and self employed	Total changes
South-East	+3.5%	+8.2%	+669,000
East Anglia	+21.2%	+26.2%	+205,000
South-West	+2.1%	+10.6%	+185,000
East Midlands	+2.4%	+7.3%	+122,000
South	+4.3%	+9.6%	+181,000
West Midlands	−4.5%	+0.1%	+2,000
Yorkshire	−7.7%	−2.6%	−56,000
North-West	−13.6%	−10.0%	−290,000
North	−9.6%	−6.3%	−84,000
Wales	−13.6%	−10.2%	−118,000
Scotland	−8.2%	−5.2%	−118,000
Northern Ireland	−6.2%	−5.7%	−34,000
North	−9.2%	−5.5%	−698,000

As the head of the industrialists' organisation, the Scottish Council (Development and Industry), said in December 1987, 'It must be a source of amazement that in some areas economic growth needs to be slowed down. There is a grave risk that the blunt instrument of high interest rates designed to cure overheating of the South-East economy will prevent some areas from even warming up.' What was needed, he argued, was a coherent and effective regional policy.

In the last ten years the economy in the South-East has grown by an average 2.3% a year, in the South-West by 3.1% and in East Anglia by 4%. In stark contrast the West Midlands, once the engine of industrial growth, grew by less than half as much — averaging 1.5% annually — Wales by only 1.4% and Scotland by 1.9%. In the North-West growth has been only 1.3% a year. Nor can the low regional growth rates be explained only by the recession immediately after 1979. Between 1981 and 1987, when Mr Lawson has spoken of six years of uninterrupted growth, the South-East has been growing 50% faster than the North-

Table 3   Average annual regional growth rates 1979–88

South-East	2.3%
East Anglia	4.0%
South-West	3.1%
East Midlands	2.7%
Northern Areas	1.6%
West Midlands	1.5%
Yorkshire and Humberside	1.9%
North-West	1.3%
North	1.8%
Wales	1.4%
Scotland	1.9%
Northern Ireland	2.2%

West. Overall, over the Thatcher ten years, the southern triangle of Britain has grown by more than 2.6%, the regions by 1.6%.

Longer term forecasts published in the recent Cambridge Econometrics/Northern Ireland Economic Research Centre review suggest that far from narrowing, the regional divide will widen in the years to 2000. Annual growth between now and the end of the 1990s is expected to be 4.1% in East Anglia and 3.8% in the South-West, but only 1.6% in the North and 1.3% in the North-West. Again one part of the economy is expected to grow at half the rate of the other, with, inevitably, renewed emigration from the North to South. One sad prediction is that one worker in every eight will emigrate from the North-West. Nearly three-quarters of a million immigrants are expected to arrive in the already congested South. The demands placed on infrastructure in the South scarcely bear contemplation: the programmes to upgrade rundown infrastructure in the North are at risk too.

Growth has been poor because investment has been inadequate. Figures are, as yet, available only for the years up to 1986. Between 1980 and 1986 the real value of productive investment has fallen by 5.9% in the West Midlands, by 10.2% in Scotland.

Ministers have told us that as manufacturing jobs disappear service jobs arise. But the unpalatable fact is that lost manufacturing jobs now outnumber new service jobs by 2 to 1. That is the figure for North and South together, but where manufacturing jobs have gone in the northern regions service jobs have gone too. Far away from the North the service sector may be enjoying a boomlet in the form of boutiques, share shops, doner kebab outlets and sauna parlours, but in the North not even the laundrettes, hamburger stands and home improvement centres can prosper as the manufacturing industries continue to languish and jobs, people and money move south.

The result is that UK (South) Ltd, which has only 42% of the population, has enjoyed nearly 60% of the increase in small businesses, won nearly 70% of all new service sector jobs and supports nearly 65% of the new self-employed the government claims to have discovered since 1979. The conclusion must surely be that the service-based secondary economy of the South offers no magic nor even any message for the problems of the North, where the primary economy has been systematically destroyed.

Official propaganda suggests that gradually the gap between the regions is narrowing, that the features of the southern economy are spreading gradually up the M1. The fact is that the longer the government has stayed in power the greater the gap has become between the fortunes of the two nations, North and South. Although the government takes great satisfaction from citing figures for increasing employment, much of it self-employment, since 1983, the figure deceives. It includes both North and South and conceals the fact that from 1983 to 1988 employment remained static in Scotland, rose by only 0.5% in the North-West and actually fell in Northern Ireland.

Figures for company registrations show that formation of new businesses has been much more rapid south of the Wash. In the North-West businesses registered for VAT have increased by only 6.8% while they have increased by 19% in the South-East. In Wales, the North and Yorkshire the increase is only of the order of 9%. Of the regions, Northern Ireland alone stands out in the creation of new enterprises, its 16% increase more or less matching that of the Home Counties. There is a simple explanation: Northern Ireland still enjoys a degree of interventionism, retaining, for example, its Local Enterprise Development Unit, something no other region has managed to do.

In the new technology industries the dominance of the South is clear. Nearly half of all employment in high technology industries is located in the South-East, largely in the Home Counties. Hertfordshire, Berkshire and Hampshire stand out as boom areas of high technology, while areas with proud industrial traditions are left behind. Most of the country's capability in research and development is clustered in the ring extending from Cambridge in East Anglia round to South Hampshire, a concentration that creates disadvantage and competitive weakness for the northern economies.

More than ever before economic power is focused in the South-East. As the end of the Eighties approaches, 60% of the top 1,000 companies have their headquarters located in London and the South-East. Mergers and takeovers exacerbate this, with the West Midlands the latest region to be hit as local firms lose their autonomy and control of them moves south.

Table 4   Location of HQs of top 1,000 UK companies

Region	1980	1988	Rel. to pop.
South-East	612	620	2.04
South-West	23	30	0.36
East Anglia	16	18	0.52
West Midlands	85	57	0.63
East Midlands	43	51	0.74
Yorkshire Humberside	64	77	0.58
North-West	77	65	0.32
North	19	17	0.90
Wales	4	10	0.20
Scotland	54	49	0.55
Northern Ireland	3	4	0.15

The widening divide that separates the shires and suburbs from the inner cities and regions expresses itself not only in job prospects but in wage levels, family incomes and in the numbers in poverty. Household incomes which averaged between £15 and £20 a week less than those in the South-East in 1979 are now up to £50 a week less. In the simplest terms, Scottish, Welsh and northern households have £55 less a week to spend on necessities than their counterparts down south. Wage rates continue to drift apart. In 1979 average wages in the North were about £10 less. Now they are £30 or £40 a week lower.

Officially, a brave new capitalism is marching outwards from the South-East, and the Midlands and the North are being reclaimed for the free market. In reality, over the last ten years 'the regions' have come to mean all the regions except one, or perhaps only part of one. The incomes of Yorkshire and Midlands households lagged behind those of the South-East by 10% in 1979. Today the gap is nearly 30% and on all the evidence it is continuing to widen.

Now as the government's own statistics on the problem can no longer be denied a new regional strategy has emerged: that of blaming the victims. Indeed, as the political price of abandoning the regions dawns on some members of the government, Tory regional policy has become a mixture of simple neglect and hypocritical moralising. Over the past few years Mr Norman Tebbit has called the wounds of the North 'self-inflicted'. Earlier, Mr John Butcher, then Minister for the North, called northerners 'workshy'. Mrs Currie, as junior Health Minister, caricatured lifestyles in the North and blamed people there for inflicting poor health upon themselves. Mrs Thatcher accused them of being 'moaning minnies'.

It is clear that the government has nothing to offer the greater part of the country except the accusation that all of its troubles are of its own making and things must get worse before they get better. In 1986 the Chancellor called for 'greater regional differentiation of pay' to encourage labour mobility. Others, such as Kenneth Clarke, have joined the call, despite all the evidence that it is not wage levels, but local investment and skills that are the critical factors in encouraging firms into the regions.

And so it goes on. If there is no investment it is because the regions lack thrift. If there is no new industry it is because their populations lack entrepreneurial initiative. Few people, and very few north of Watford, can be persuaded to believe this, but the more the government's regional policy failures are exposed the more ministers seek to blame the victims of their economic assault. Not only have two nations been created, one has been set against the other.

The major decision was the one to downgrade and eventually eliminate regional aid. This more than anything else has served to widen the gap. In 1979 regional aid was worth £251 million for Scotland. It is now worth £107 million. For Wales in 1979 it was worth £209 million. It is now worth £104 million. Regional aid in England amounted to £608 million ten years ago but is now worth only £247 million.

Automatic regional development grants have now been abandoned despite all the evidence that they had created substantial numbers of jobs. A recent report on the withdrawal of such incentives from the Edinburgh area found that 49% of companies had reduced expenditure as a result and 33% were considering moving. The report concluded that the impact on investment and employment 'could be significantly greater in the long term'. Yet the report was issued by the government with a press release entitled 'Regional incentive withdrawal caused no marked drop in the local economies'.

What of the future? Some Tories are concerned. Despite their differences on certain topics both Leon Brittan and Michael Heseltine have been strident in their demands for an active regional policy. Leon Brittan has gone so far as to call the 'gulf between different parts of the country unjust and divisive. I believe that we can and that the government should do more to help.' And Michael Heseltine, talking of the North, has regretted the 'tragic journey downwards. There is no cause to justify underprivileged parts of England sliding much further into despair, apparently supposed to fight their corners unarmed against the forces of industrial decline.'

Heseltine's answer is intervention. 'Where is the logic of the exclusion of overwhelming demand for public investment . . . No Tory government has ever believed that unfettered capitalism would inevitably deliver a social purpose or that the product of unfettered capitalism was necessarily fair' (23 June 1986).

He could have qualified that a little: 'No Tory government until that of Mrs Thatcher'. And its attitude to the growing wage gap is both characteristic and illuminating. The government demands simply that it widens still further. Their solution, that of regionally varied wage rates, is already applied in many industries. Now they seek to extend it to the public sector. The problem is that it is unlikely to achieve its professed objective, that of creating jobs on a scale that will reduce unemployment elsewhere.

Nowhere has the impact of neglect and underinvestment over the Thatcher years been greater than in the inner cities. Nowhere is there starker evidence of the consequences of giving free rein to market forces. All this received belated recognition from Mrs Thatcher on the night of the 1987 election when she told party workers that 'something had to be done for the inner cities'.

Market forces have played a large part in precipitating the decline of our inner cities. In manufacturing, changing floorspace requirements and access needs have made inner city locations increasingly unattractive in comparison with greenfield sites adjacent to small towns. And as industry has moved out growing dereliction in the inner cities has depressed land values and deterred redevelopment. Vast tracts of the inner cities have degenerated to industrial wasteland that is costly to clear and redevelop.

Local communities become increasingly unbalanced as the tax base declines and service demands rise as a consequence of mounting social problems. Once decline sets in, bad gets rapidly worse. Problems accumulate, wealth drains away. And such communities have suffered even more harshly as a result of the UK government's intensifying assault on local government. Money necessary for the regeneration of the inner cities has been denied them.

Despite avowals that 'something must be done', Treasury support for inner city projects has fallen substantially. Funding for Mrs Thatcher's crusade on the inner cities has turned out to be a window-dressing exercise, a reshuffling and republicising of existing and generally inadequate grant arrangements. Grants for the reclamation of derelict land, for the urban programme, for the city programme and for urban development corporations have been re-packaged and passed off as largesse. And to crown an astonishing exercise in cynicism, the value of these grants will actually fall next year, and the next, and the next after that.

Regional grants, the main source of industrial cash for the cities of the North, are already worth £500 million less than they were in 1979 and will fall by a further £150 million by 1992. Between this year and next the rate support grant for the most difficult inner city areas partnership and programme authorities will fall yet again. Friends of the Earth reported recently that Manchester had lost £350 million in rate support grant and gained less than £10 million in increased urban programme spending.

Even where jobs have been created inadequate local training opportunities have meant that few local people have been in a position to benefit. Even when 10,000 jobs were being created by the London Docklands Development Corporation local unemployment was rising and is still much higher. As one Tory Reform Group member explained, they were 'perturbed' by the attitude of the London Docklands Development Corporation which had 'in two and a half years not thought to enquire what had happened to the over 40,000 Londoners who had once lived in the area'. Overall inner city unemployment figures have fallen more slowly than those elsewhere.

And as jobs have failed to appear, both private and public funding initiatives are the subject of official exaggeration. Government hype puts private investment four times higher than cold reality would allow. It is scarcely surprising that nothing much has happened. As the Town and Country Planning Association pointed out in January, 'In the inner city areas and elsewhere the government's regeneration policies are working too slowly to help those in need'.

In the inner cities more than anywhere else is seen the need for a public role in redevelopment and modernisation. While the social benefits of redevelopment are obvious, there are stages in regeneration that are quite simply not capable of yielding sufficient return on private investment to make them attractive or even viable for commercial developers. Whether in the form of garden festivals or enterprise zones or inner city task forces of Urban Development Corporations, publicly funded intervention is required.

Any misguided conviction that an answer will be found simply by opening the inner cities to market forces can be refuted by the manifest lack of progress over the years during which this has been tried, could have happened and hasn't. Even government ministers now have to accept that. The problem is that, as with the regions, the inner cities cannot flourish without a level of public investment and strategic intervention that the government, so far at least, has been unwilling to contemplate.

The Triumph of Commercial Greed

7

How Consumers Lost Out

Mr David Clark. To ask the Minister of Agriculture, Fisheries and Food how many meetings he or his ministerial colleagues have had in 1988 with:
a) The National Farmers Union
b) The Royal Society for the Protection of Birds
c) The Council for the Protection of Rural England
d) The Royal Society for Nature Conservation
e) The World Wide Fund for Nature
f) The Friends of the Earth
g) The National Consumer Council
h) Consumers in the European Community Group
i) The London Food Commission
j) The United Kingdom Agricultural Supply Trade Association

Mr MacGregor . . . the number of identifiable formal ministerial meetings which ministers had during 1988 which included national representatives of the organisations listed was:
a) 37   b) 4   c) 2   d) 0   e) 0   f) 0   g) 2   h) 0   i) 1   j) 7 . . . .

Hansard, written answer 16 January 1989

British consumers have fared badly over the last ten years. Perhaps they should not have expected otherwise: the word 'consumer' did not appear at all in the Tory manifestoes of 1979 and 1983. In 1987 consumer affairs merited only a 10-word sentence which read: 'But competition must be supplemented by legal protection for consumers.' Not much was promised, and less was delivered. Indeed one of the first actions of the 1979 Tory government in the field of consumer rights was to get rid of the Department of Prices and Consumer Protection. Consumers' Advice Centres have been closed and over the last five years the number of officials charged with protecting the consumers' interest — Trading Standards Officers and Environmental Health Officers — has fallen by 330. While in Norway and New Zealand consumers have a Ministry of Consumer Affairs to protect their interests and in most EEC countries consumer rights are clear and clearly enforcible, UK consumers have actually lost rights and protection over the 1980s.

It is not that British consumers do not stand in need of protection. Over the last ten years the number of people seeking help from Citizens' Advice Bureaux has gone up by 3.5 million to 7.6 million. Every year thousands of people suffer disfigurement, injury or death from unsafe products. Children are particularly at risk: 7,800 are poisoned by household chemicals; 9,600 injured by unlaminated glass doors, 2,400 burnt by oven doors. Thousands of people find themselves the victims of misleading advertising and information. Each year it is estimated three-quarters of a million people are dissatisfied about the holiday that did not turn out the way the brochure had promised, and one-and-a-half million motorists are dissatisfied with the performance of the car they have bought or had serviced. Thousands injured by medical drugs find the pursuit of proper redress in Britain a slow and disappointing struggle.

Were it not for the EEC the situation would be even worse. On those few occasions when the Tories have moved to strengthen consumer interests they have done so at the behest of the European Commission, have done so reluctantly and have often done so only after exercising every conceivable means of delaying and diluting the intended harmonisation of consumer protection legislation. The EEC has pushed through directive after directive. The British government and the vested interests it represents have spent much of the last ten years fighting off community regulations that would have greatly helped the British consumer. In a now familiar sequence of events, the British government contests new legislation in Brussels, loses, resorts then to delaying tactics, attempts to obtain a derogation — which would allow a national exemption — then requests a protracted period for implementation and finally either fails to implement the legislation or waters it down to the point of ineffectiveness.

Food standards are a particular cause for concern. Salmonella food poisoning notifications have gone up from 9,000 to 17,000 in the nine years to 1987, although even that alarming figure is widely seen as a gross underestimate. The problem is that the notification rate is a small but unknown fraction of the true incidence which, some experts consider, may even be as high as two million a year. When the salmonella in eggs crisis broke the real disarray of British consumer protection was amply demonstrated. Rather than a strong department with the remit of consumer protection taking charge, two departments, one virtually a producer lobby, drifted aimlessly until public embarrassment compelled Prime Ministerial action. And that action? It did not result in a clean up of the industry — powerful lobbies are involved — but in a decision that it is the consumer who must take responsibility, with the issue of four million leaflets on the subject of food hygiene.

The message is clear. The government is not committed to ensuring that food on sale is safe, but prefers to distribute blame and advice that implies that unsafe food will be freely available and that consumers must be responsible for ensuring that unsafe food does not damage their health. And even then consumers must struggle with the inadequate and misleading labelling of food that government policy has sought to maintain despite considerable pressure from Europe. The EEC decided in its framework directive 79/112/EEC on the date stamping of food that produce and products should be labelled clearly with a 'USE BEFORE' date. The government, under pressure from the highly organised and influential food industry lobby, denied the British public the clarity and safety of the European standard, opting instead for a 'SELL BY' date of much less value in food hygiene. What does it matter when food is to be sold by? What matters is when it is safe to eat. The Trading Standards Officers pointed this out to the government in 1983. They were ignored.

According to Mrs Thatcher the food problem is almost no problem at all. When Neil Kinnock questioned her on food safety she replied that 'the government has enabled the consumer to have a wider choice of food at all price ranges than ever before, and we have taken active steps to ensure that the consumer has the information to choose food to meet their personal preferences and lifestyle'. What that means is that the government has followed the line of the food industry and opted for a 'move away from compositional standards to more information on the labels'. The government has decided against banning food additives — colours and preservatives — already forbidden in many countries on

85

grounds of risk, and left it to the industry to use them as it wishes, provided that some rather uninformative information is displayed almost illegibly on the tin or wrapper. Once again the consumer is left with the unwelcome responsibility of incomplete information and possibly unsafe food.

In the words of Caroline Walker, 'The trouble with this policy, which superficially suggests that both industry and consumers should be more free, is that it allows manufacturers to put whatever is good for business into their products as long as they own up in the small print. Critics fear that the abandonment of compositional standards could only lead to the legalised further debasement of food.' There are good grounds for such fears, as previous experience has shown that if regulations are weakened food quality quickly falls. In 1987 the government eased standards on some meat products. A study of 22 sample products showed that the meat content dropped in every case. The average meat content under the old standards would have been 46.8%. It fell to 31.3%. The less regulated market drove quality down and choice did not increase: higher meat content products were no longer on offer.

Unfortunately for the consumer, the completion of the internal market in 1992 is likely to make food worse rather than better. Originally the plan was to devise standards, safe and universally applicable, in the way that has been achieved for toys. But food standardisation has been frustrated by difficulties over definitions and in reaching agreement on common rules for each type of product (even chocolate has caused problems). Faced with years of wrangling, the EEC backed off and a new policy is proposed: in future if a product can be legally sold in any one member country then the 11 other member states will have to allow it to be sold unless they can convince the Commission on grounds of risk to health, safety, the environment or consumer protection that it ought to be excluded.

Instead of standardisation there will be a 'well-developed and clear system of labelling, presentation and advertising . . . so that the producer may be protected against unfair competition and consumers against misleading practice'. Labelling offers doubtful protection to the consumers. How many of them will appreciate the nuances opened up by such terms as 'bacon crisps', 'bacon flavoured crisps' and 'bacon-flavour crisps'? (Hint: the last has nothing to do with bacon

86

at all.) Blandly titled bulking agents and mysterious numbers will loom large. European food standards will be lowered to the lowest common denominator by this 'legal anywhere, legal everywhere' approach and as things stand the UK may become, for the food industry, Europe's softest option, the land where anything goes. This is because food labelling regulations and standards for additives here are subject to scarcely any public scrutiny and are decided largely by industrial interests, with the independent consumer voice usually shouted down.

The food additive committees of the UK come under the Official Secrets Act and are subject also to very considerable pressure from the food industry lobby, since a lot of money is to be made by adding cheap chemicals to even cheaper basic foodstuffs: the flavouring and texturing of soya protein to resemble meat is an obvious and lucrative example. Expert advice to these committees is likely to be financed by companies with much to gain from a favourable decision and industry members may actually outnumber the scientists and lay members added together. Inevitably public and consumer suspicions are great. As Leslie Yeomans of the Consumers' Association told a meeting of the Society of the Chemical Industry: 'You fought for a long time to keep additives off food labels. If you're suffering from a backlash from consumers, you have only yourselves to blame.'

The government has done little to set things right. The 1984 Food Act, a consolidating measure bringing together all the existing legislation, was not seen as an opportunity to improve on standards of food safety and hygiene, though it could have been. The Institute of Environmental Health felt let down when powers to act on food safety problems at source were denied them, and factories remain virtually immune from their attentions. The government's attitude to European attempts to improve food standards has been almost entirely negative: opposing new legislation that controls hormone use in the meat industry; seeking derogations on dubious and dangerous food additives; failing to implement standards of protection in the area of dairy products.

There is nothing mysterious about why a government should be so careless of the interests of its citizens. For the Tories, food industry profits matter a lot more than food standards. Not much has changed since Lord Boyd Orr, Britain's greatest nutritionist, wrote in 1936: 'If children of the three lower income groups were reared for profit like young animals giving them a diet below the requirements for health would be financially unsound. Unfortunately, the health and fitness of the rising generation are not marketable commodities which can be assessed in terms of value for money.' And what hope now for improved food standards from a party lobbied (and heavily financed) by the food industry and led by a woman whose early career as a food chemist included the task of working out how to put as much air as possible, in the form of little bubbles, into Joe Lyons' ice-cream? Costs down, profits up, the public bamboozled: as senior politicians go, Mrs Thatcher has unique experience of the practical side of British food standards.

Consumer interests other than food are watched over by a junior minister at the Department of Trade (now known as the Department of Enterprise). The current incumbent, a Mr Eric Forth, is not exactly a household name, and nothing is known about him that might lead consumers to believe that their interests are being watched over with any enthusiasm. Mr Forth is currently engaged in a struggle to stop the EEC implementing a new draft directive to protect holidaymakers who find themselves the victims of unscrupulous tour operators. The EEC intends to legislate to make tour firms liable for flight delays, overbooked hotels and surcharges. Public feeling on these issues is high and the Consumers' Association has gone on record as saying that, 'It is simply unacceptable that so many people get holidays that are clearly not the package they paid for. We considered the original draft directive a major step forward for consumers.'

By European standards the British holidaymaker enjoys poor protection and, according to Trading Standards Officers, is more likely to have something to complain about than his German, French or Italian neighbours. In the words of LACOTS, the coordinating body for Trading Standards Officers: 'Despite the enormous scale of the holiday industry, the UK is behind several other European Member States in relation to establishing specific legislation on the holiday trade. Belgium, France, Italy, Portugal and Spain have all introduced specific laws which define the rights of the consumer and the obligations of the tour operators . . . The British consumer is generally at a disadvantage when compared to his/her counterpart in several member states where there are more specific laws.'

At present if a British holidaymaker gets food poisoning in Sicily or is injured when a hotel balcony collapses in Cyprus he is advised that his official route to a remedy is by individually suing the hotelier via the local courts. None but the brave, rich or very determined would be much inclined to try. The consumer movement argues that 'tour operators are in a stronger position than the individual holidaymaker to recover damages from foreign hotels or transport carriers, since they can withdraw from future bookings. Consumers should get what they pay for. Holidays are paid for unseen, in advance. If expectations are sometimes unrealistic they are expectations created by the tour operators themselves, operators who often refuse to accept any responsibility for their product.'

The draft directive proposed by the EEC and opposed by Mr Forth would help holidaymakers a lot. A proper description of what is on offer, information to allow comparisons, protection against late or hidden surcharges and adequate redress when things go wrong would take a lot of the worry and uncertainty out of a purchase which, after housing and cars, is the largest item in many a family budget. Complaints are common and Trading Standards Officers, the public officials who have to pick up the pieces, feel that only a change in the law will help. 'There is no specific UK holiday legislation to protect consumers and therefore complaints have to be pursued under more general civil and criminal law, the provisions of which are not always adequate to deal with the dishonest or negligent trader.' But the consumer will look in vain to a Tory government for help in achieving any progress.

The government argues that increasing regulation will increase costs and mean an end to cheap holidays, even though this has not happened elsewhere in Europe. ABTA, the holiday trade association, has lobbied vigorously to head off consumer protection of proven value and maintain the present vulnerability of the individual British holidaymaker. Despite survey findings that 3% of holidays are 'spoiled by problems' and another 6% caused dissatisfaction, ABTA is complacent, both about the holidays it provides and about its lobbying efforts. In material sent to all MPs it states: 'ABTA is encouraged by the recent decision of the Council of Tourism Ministers to refer back the Directive to its authors in the Commission in Brussels . . . ABTA also welcomes the government's rejecting a licensing system for the travel trade . . . The Association will, however, continue to press for the achievement of an equitable balance between the interests of consumers and its members.' And Her Majesty's Government will, it seems, continue to support the commercial lobby at the expense of the consumer.

The case of product liability demonstrates another mechanism whereby British consumers are denied the advantages of European initiatives. In this instance legislation offering full protection got through the EEC but was quietly neutered by the Tory government in the implementation phase by the use of a loophole in European procedures. The EEC began with the idea that a manufacturer's liability for defective products should be strict (i.e. proof without fault) and not based on negligence as under the law that existed then. In UK law a person who was injured or suffered damage could bring only an action based on contract or negligence, and the consumer had to prove that the manufacturer was negligent.

The concept of product liability grew from cases such as the thalidomide tragedy and was intended to spare the victims having to fight for compensation through the courts. The CBI opposed the idea on the grounds that product liability would increase business costs, especially insurance costs in such high-risk areas as pharmaceuticals, chemicals and aerospace, and reduce the competitiveness of British companies. According to the CBI product liability would also put small companies out of business, cause job losses, inhibit innovation and reduce consumer choice. A long and bitter argument over the directive followed, and eventually, to get agreement of some sort, the EEC had to introduce a less rigorous variant for member states who wanted a way out of strict product liability.

The agreed directive allowed an option for member states by which their own legislation might include a development risks defence: in essence waiving liability for producers who could prove that the state of scientific and technical knowledge at the relevant time was not such as to enable the existence of a defect to be discovered. Its application to such cases as the thalidomide tragedy is as obvious as it is unacceptable to consumers. The UK government fought product liability for years but the product liability directive was finally enacted by the EEC in 1985. Once that had happened the CBI concentrated its efforts on making sure that when the directive was implemented in UK legislation the development risk clause was not only there but defined with maximum latitude, in practice virtually unlimited.

The consumer organisations fought development risks defence

The argument that the producer could not have foreseen injurious effects might be interpreted widely and to the great detriment of consumer interests, in effect allowing safety trials to be conducted on an unconsenting public. The Consumers' Association, the National Consumer Council, the Pearson Commission and the Law Commission all took the view that the producers should not be allowed the development risks defence. If it were included the only significant difference between the existing position and the new law would be the transfer of the burden of proving negligence. In future the producer would have to prove he was not negligent instead of the victim having to prove he was.

When the bill was published it contained the widest development risks defence possible. The House of Lords did not succeed in dropping the development risks clause but did amend it to achieve the narrower wording of the EEC original. And significantly the Lords almost succeeded in passing an amendment preventing drug companies from using the development risks defence. When the bill went back to the Commons the government made no attempt to reverse their Lordships' amendment, but waited until the committee stage where, in the words of Baroness Burton, 'government draftsmen softened the demands made upon UK producers, introducing more wishy-washy concepts' and without even taking a committee vote reinstated wording which the CBI briefing had argued 'will make it easier for a company to mount the defence of development risks'. Lord Allen concluded: 'I do not think the government will be able to look with any pride in their surrender to the arguments of industry' — industry in this context including pharmaceuticals.

The long struggle of patients treated with the Eli Lilly drug Opren illustrates just how little protection British law really offers. US courts — and Eli Lilly is a US company — ruled strict liability and US victims were by 1986 being awarded up to $6 million each. British victims fought for five years after the drug was withdrawn, by which time many were frail and some had died, running substantial risks of huge legal costs, and eventually the company offered victims an average of £2,000 each. One woman, Miss Kathleen Graham, who led the fight for compensation, said: 'The long and vastly expensive legal fight has resulted in a settlement offer. I must emphasise it is legal; but today the poor, the sick and the old can see exactly where

they stand in regard to British law.' The broader fight continues
On 22 December 1988 the EEC commission, following complaint
from the Consumers' Association that the UK had not implemented
the directive on product liability as intended, announced that it wa
starting infringement procedures against the British government.

The much-criticised 1987 Consumer Protection Act has among it
other failings a clause devised more for the protection of producer
than consumers. This clause allows a manufacturer to use a 'produc
standard' to defend himself or herself from claims of negligence in
court. At first reading this sounds reasonable but the details ar
somewhat disquieting. Standards are determined not by consumers an
safety experts but by technical committees dominated by trade interests
Over a thousand committees, organised under the aegis of the Britis
Standards Institution and hence the DTI, are involved. Consumer
and Trading Standards Officers sit, but are outnumbered by industr
representation. Committee papers are secret, as are committee ses
sions. Thus are the standards defined whereby manufacturers defen
themselves when accused of negligence.

One alarming example of the consumer protection afforded b
this system is enough. For 20 years the Consumers' Association ha
been campaigning for a reduction in the maximum permitted outsid
temperature for domestic cookers. Every home has a cooker and man
homes have children. Oven doors may legally be much hotter, at 12
degrees centigrade, than boiling water, and many burns to small childre
and others result. Yet the Association of Manufacturers of Domesti
Electrical Appliances and the Society of British Gas Industries hav
used the product standard and the committee system to resist pressure
for increased consumer protection for two decades.

Another important area where consumer protection is not only wea
but getting weaker is that of consumer credit and debt collection. Th
1974 Consumer Credit Act imposed a requirement on debt collectio
agencies to obtain a licence, thus ensuring a vetting process and
means of control using withdrawal of the licence as an ultimat
sanction. The UK government, putting the best possible face on it
consumer protection measures for an OECD inquiry, boasted that i
1985–86 270 licensees or applicants had been examined and man
found unfit to hold licences.

That was most reassuring, but in 1988 a DTI discussion documen proposed that the requirement on debt collectors to hold a licence should be withdrawn. The reasoning was as follows: many licences had been issued (around 200,000), many of them to small firms with limited resources, and in only a few instances (around 900) had there been 'adverse determinations'. The Department therefore felt that it had 'imposed a disproportionate burden on the great majority of law-abiding businesses' and proposed a 'more flexible and appropriate system of control'.

Others have grave doubts. Sir Gordon Borrie, the Director General of the Office of Fair Trading, immediately attacked the proposals on the grounds that many of the worst abuses relating to credit agreements have resulted from the activities of debt collectors. The National Chairman of the Institute of Trading Standards Officers, Mr Bob Wright, felt that deregulation would deprive Trading Standards Officers of the single most effective weapon at their disposal and encourage 'bomb site operators' who might operate briefly and crudely and escape effective control.

And after ten years of Tory government many more people are liable to be visited by a debt collector. No detailed figures exist, but bankruptcies have doubled since 1979 and warrant sales increased by over 50%. Although lenders and hirers would still need to be licensed, credit brokers, debt collectors and others acting merely as agents for lenders would not. Are deregulated debt collectors, about their business visiting the homes of people already vulnerable, really expected to refrain consistently from the 'worst abuses' already noted by Sir Gordon Borrie?

After ten years of consumer protection, Tory-style, the message is clear. The government is much more inclined to listen to the arguments of its friends in industry, its generous friends in industry, its friends in industry who claim to know what the consumers want and who insist that any consumer protection legislation beyond the most anodyne and bland will damage industry, raise prices and reduce consumer choice. There are many cruel examples of how this accord works in practice and how consumers thus patronised by industry and denied their rights by government have suffered. And the lady who worked on selling air-bubbles as ice cream is unlikely to have a change of heart simply because she has just become a grandmother.

8

Privatisation: Who Benefits?

'We have said clearly to the government that unless and until it is adequately regulated, simply moving a monopoly from the public to the private sector does little or nothing for its customers. Robust regulation of the privatised industry will be needed if consumers are not to be faced with rising prices and falling standards.'
Former Tory MP, Mrs Sally Oppenheim Barnes, Financial Times, *July 1988*

Mrs Oppenheim Barnes, the Tory-appointed chairman of the Consumers' Council, was the first to speak of the privatised industries as operating 'a black market' where prices could be forced up at will and consumers had little power to influence prices or standards. Yet the government's policy for consumers has for the most part been simply one of privatisation and more privatisation. As a later chapter will show, there has been no substantial extension of consumer rights, no new right of redress for consumers, no new right to refund or right of representation, no guidelines or legislation for improved service or improved consumer safeguards and little in the way of improved safety standards. Nor has there been any attempt to curb the production and sale of shoddy, badly designed, poorly finished goods. Indeed there has been very little attempt to stand up for ordinary people against the vested interests of business and vast corporations. In the last ten years the power of the ordinary consumer against those interests has not been increased but diminished.

Criticism of the government's failure in the field of consumer rights has been deflected or simply shouted down in the propaganda barrage attendant upon the various privatisation initiatives. The government claims repeatedly that its historic transfer of assets from public to private ownership has been a great achievement for consumer interests. All consumers, we are told, will benefit from privatisation because of the increased efficiency generated by means of increased competition.

The facts are very different. In many cases the government has quite cynically transformed a public monopoly into a private one, without any stipulations that might increase or just maintain consumer rights. In general, consumer safeguards, despite the rhetoric, have featured very low in the government's priorities during its privatisation drive.

It is worth looking in detail at what has happened to consumer rights in the brave new world of privatisation. What has happened to the consumer's right to an efficient service? In the case of British Telecom huge claims were made for a higher standard and quality of service by Cecil Parkinson, the then Industry Minister.

'More important, it will give customers the choice between different suppliers of apparatus, different suppliers of services and increasingly different networks.'

'I am convinced that the change in BT ownership will bring about a major improvement in BT's accountability . . . in future BT will be accountable to its shareholders . . . to its customers, to OFTEL and to its bankers and it will be subject to competition.'

'BT's licence will forbid it to discriminate between different categories of customer.'

'We offer millions of BT customers a newly enshrined set of rights and benefits of competition and new technology.'

In practice what has happened to British Telecom has been very different. Post-privatisation BT is less accountable rather than more. The effective competition promised is largely fiction, since in most places BT enjoys a monopoly. Business users are favoured over domestic customers and millions of telephone users remain unconvinced about any newly enshrined set of rights and benefits.

Services have deteriorated. Despite a formal price freeze charges have gone up. The new services that have been introduced have come in at a hefty cost to the consumer. British Telecom charges new telephone users £16, which is said to cover reconnection and the updating of its own records, and makes £50 million a year by doing so. There have been new charges for priority repair services for doctors, nurses, policemen and ambulancemen. The useful, such as directory enquiries — now slow and often inaccessible and which may soon cost 30p — has been neglected in favour of the profitable, such as commercial soft-porn chatlines — with profits 30% of turnover.

BT's much-trumpeted price freeze has camouflaged a system of charges that has forced domestic prices up faster than those for business users. International comparisons reveal how disadvantaged the British home telephone user has become. According to the most recent National Utility Survey, the cost of making a local telephone call within Britain is the second highest in the world. Only in Australia, at 9.9p for a three-minute local call, is it higher. Such a call in the UK costs 9.8p. Third most expensive is in Belgium at only 7.4p.

Tariff charges are high, but bills may be even higher because of overcharging. This is a huge problem and the completely itemised bills which might provide safeguards against it will not be fully available until the mid-1990s. Meanwhile, BT has achieved the unique and dubious distinction among the privatised companies of being able to charge for services of which the customer may sometimes have no knowledge.

The consumer remains at a grave disadvantage. As the National Consumers' Council concluded, 'The regulatory régime formally sets prices without reference to costs. Any reduction in BT's costs will be translated straight into profit. This is deliberately contrived to give managers an incentive to improve efficiency. It can also, however, provide an incentive to reduce the quality of the service. This is perhaps the most serious defect in the regulatory system. *At best it provides no positive encouragement to improve services. At worst it actually pulls in the opposite direction.*'

But no action has been taken on excess profits. As OFTEL has seen, BT's rate of return exceeds 20%. This high profitability has not, however, resulted in adequate investment. Over the last few years BT's investment record has lagged behind those of most other international communications companies. According to an OECD survey of 13 countries, BT has spent least on new investment between 1983 and 1985.

Nor has privatised British Telecom succeeded in meeting generally agreed social objectives. Although since 1983 there has been a rebate scheme limiting rental charges for low income users (under which those using less than 120 units per quarter could enjoy a 30% rebate on their rental), BT has forced domestic charges up, taking rebated rental up too, while at the same time offering preferential pricing for commercial and industrial users. The social objectives previously recognised are not among BT's priorities, and accordingly information on them is no longer kept.

Although lucrative new telephone boxes are appearing everywhere, many homes, especially those of the elderly, go without phones. Again international comparisons are illuminating. Britain still has fewer homes with telephones than is the case in most comparable nations. With only 524 per 1,000 inhabitants, Britain is behind the USA (760), France (608), Germany (621), Sweden (890), Switzerland (832), Japan (555), New Zealand (672) and Australia (551). Curiously, only Iceland, with 525 per 1,000 inhabitants, is in our league.

Qualitatively, quantitatively and in terms of price our telephone service is now less than satisfactory. This is reflected in survey data. In 1980 54% considered British Telecom's prices reasonable. By 1987 only 34% did. By that time 26% found repair work unsatisfactory, and on that evidence and by other measures of how it dealt with customers British Telecom was found to be worse than other utilities then still in the public sector. One in six BT customers queried their bills in the two years to November 1987. Generally, as another 1986 survey found, more people thought that British Telecom's service had deteriorated since privatisation than thought that it had improved.

In the view of the National Consumers' Council the BT licence is unsatisfactory in many different ways. 'The contract is one-sided in the extreme . . . other clauses give BT the unrestricted right to alter a customer's telephone number, to demand a deposit of any size at any time and to pay interest on that deposit at the company's discretion and at a rate that it decides; to avoid liability for anything the company might do or fail to do . . . OFTEL has no direct power over its content.'

The truth is that BT as a licence holder is virtually immune from being penalised for breaching licence conditions. British Telecom is on record as dismissing OFTEL as 'merely an advisory body which has no statutory powers to impose fines or revoke operating licences'. And the stated goal of improving competition remains as far off as ever. As one right-wing critic points out, the government has failed to carry out its duty to promote effective competition in the telecommunications industry. There has been 'a clear breach' of the underlying policy of competition.

The same claims of improved service and consumer rights were made for British Gas at the time of its privatisation. 'Rather than being under the constant pressure of Whitehall and the current politician in charge,' Mr Peter Walker avowed, 'it is far better in the interests of the country to ensure that commercial managers have charge over these industries.'

Privatised as a monopoly although as yet, because of falling oil prices, to be tested on its pricing policies, the British Gas structure 'has even greater infirmities than the early Telecom scheme', according to one expert. To the gas supply monopoly Mr Walker is alleged to have added 'an information monopoly. This helped the share price but not the consumer.'

There have been some changes. British Gas has lost its *de facto* position as sole purchaser of gas from the UK sector of the North Sea. Its pipelines must be open to competitors and it has been forced to reveal the profitability of its industrial effort. Direct benefits to the consumer, however, have been very few.

In some respects things have become worse. Disconnections of customers in arrears rose by 60% in the first year after privatisation and by 25% the following year. Last year's fall of 25%, much publicised for the benefit of the corporate image, still leaves disconnections far above pre-privatisation levels. Social security changes are one explanation but as the Gas Consumers' Council has reported, 'some aspects of British Gas policy also contribute'. In the case of the British Airports Authority, 'the lack of regulation on these markets allows airport operators to act at least in the short term as unconstrained monopolists,' said one report.

There is a general problem of providing protection for consumers in privatised near-monopolies. As we have seen, the OFTEL model offers little encouragement. The National Consumers' Council has laid down principles that it believes should be addressed. Consumer bodies should be independent of the regulator, unlike OFTEL, which combines regulatory and consumer watchdog responsibilities. More than that, 'there must be regulatory control of both prices and quality. The regulatory process should be an open one . . . the firms being regulated should have a duty to abide by the regulatory rules . . . the regulator should have powers to determine whether or not the regulatory rules have been broken . . . the firms being regulated should have a strict duty to supply customers.' It seems that nothing less than Mrs Oppenheim

PRIVATISATION: WHO BENEFITS?

Barnes' 'robust regulations' will do. Meanwhile there is no convincing evidence that consumers have benefited from privatisation. Indeed their rights seem far less certain now than formerly.

If privatisation has failed the consumer has it succeeded in another of its stated aims, that of popularising shareholding? Undoubtedly shares were bought and gains were made, especially in the first few days of each new issue, when quick money was there for those who bought and sold quickly. But that is not so much a success for popular capitalism as one for state-subsidised licensed betting.

In truth Mrs Thatcher's shareowning democracy is more illusion than reality. Even the Treasury's own survey shows that six out of every seven citizens hold no share in privatised companies. When Rolls Royce was privatised 52% of the shares were resold on the first day of trading, many to the Japanese. 91% of those who bought Amersham, the first privatisation, have now sold out. In the case of British Airways the figure is 68% and in the case of Jaguar 74%. In the case of British Gas 1.6 million shareholders have sold out and in the case of British Telecom 1 million. Overall nearly 40% of the shares bought up in privatisation stocks, 7.34 million shares in total, have been sold on. Among lower income groups popular capitalism is almost non-existent: only 2% of the poorest one-third of the population own any shares at all.

Table 1   Shareholders in privatisation stocks

Company	Successful applicants (thousands)	Jan. 1989	% sold shares
Amersham Int.	65	6	91
Assoc. British Ports	53	10	81
BAA	2187	1000	54
British Aerospace	415	106	74
British Airways	1100	350	68
British Gas	4407	2800	36
BT	2300	1300	44
Britoil	485	179	63
Cable & Wireless	280	182	35
Enterprise Oil	14	10	29
Jaguar	125	33	74
Rolls Royce	2000	850	58
TSB	3000	1800	40

WHERE THERE IS GREED...

Equity investment appears to have remained a static fraction of personal savings in Britain while it has actually risen substantially in France and Italy. The much vaunted Personal Equity Plan, the brainchild of Nigel Lawson, sought to extend personal shareholding by offering tax relief as an incentive. 500,000 PEPs were anticipated in the first year. In fact only 200,000 were set up, with an even more disappointing 50,000 in the second. No one knows how many have been abandoned, but the April 1989 changes in the scheme reflect the Chancellor's anxieties about the extent to which PEPs had been functioning not to recruit new shareholders in the army of popular capitalism, but to provide for those already participating some additional tax shelter facilities.

Certainly the big City institutions have done little to retain new shareholders or to make life easier for them. It is now accepted that on the day of the Stock Exchange crash in November 1987 many small investors were unable to get through to dealers with orders to sell, and institutions were reluctant to help them. Even now small investors are offered third-class services at first-class rates. A survey of attitudes to them among the top 150 City firms found a reluctance to become involved with them. One-third of firms refused to deal and another third would deal only at minimum rates of commission that were so high that the entire capital gain on shares would be wiped out. Minimum commissions, exclusive of VAT, would be above £20 in more than 75% of companies even for the smallest transfer of shares.

The net result is that control has moved to the big institutions and overseas. Less than 12% of British Telecom, for example, is now owned by the public. To date 40% of Jaguar and 15% of British Aerospace have ended up in the hands of foreigners. Control of the Royal Dockyard at Plymouth has passed to the American company Brown and Root. The foreign shareholding in Rolls Royce, whose defence contribution is vital, reached an illegal figure of 21% and, embarrassingly for patriotic privatisation enthusiasts, subsequently had to be reduced under a golden share provision.

The role of the Kuwaiti government in post-privatisation BP is well known, and potentially at odds with British interests. The Kuwaitis owned nearly 20% of BP before an elaborate buy-back deal was arranged. Figures for foreign ownership of British Telecom and British Gas are not readily available, but are believed to be approaching 10%.

PRIVATISATION: WHO BENEFITS?

The grim fact is that more of the ownership of these major companies is in foreign hands than at home under popular capitalism.

But were the interests of the ordinary shareholder ever really meant to come first? The argument for mass capitalism was produced by the Conservatives as an afterthought and only when the claims for efficiency through competition became untenable. Back in 1979 their manifesto said little about privatisation, concentrating on their opposition to Labour's plans to nationalise more firms. Once in office they sold off Amersham and other small government holdings. It was in their 1983 manifesto that privatisation was first extolled as a means of promoting competition.

At that time the Conservatives rejected any notion of privatising public utilities as monopolies. They would 'take steps to ensure that these firms do not exploit their powerful positions to the detriment of their competitors'. In 1983 the minister in charge of privatisation went even further, arguing that 'the primary objective of the government's privatisation programme is to reduce the power of the monopolist and to encourage competition . . . The long term success of the privatisation programme will stand or fall by the extent to which it maximises competition . . . If competition cannot be achieved an historic opportunity will have been lost.' A little later, however, he was saying that 'industries such as water do not depend for their success on the practice of product competition . . . This would make no sense and indeed would lead to a loss of economic efficiency and produce poorer services for the consumer.' Later, in 1985, he put it more starkly. 'I firmly believe that where competition is impractical privatisation programmes have now developed to such an extent that regulated private ownership of the monopolies is preferable to nationalisation.'

At a stroke the idea of improvement of services through competition, the entire justification for the privatisation programme, was dropped. Not only was it dropped, but a new notion suddenly arose: where public utilities were concerned competition could be positively harmful. Another justification was required, and by the time the 1987 manifesto appeared it had been identified: the aim of privatisation was wider share ownership.

Popular capitalism is a resounding slogan, but the briefest acquaint-anceship with the succession of ideas used to defend privatisation reveals its true status. The idea of competition survived only as long as

the realities permitted. As the impracticality of any real competition in
the sale of such products as gas and electricity became obvious, and as
concession after concession was made to vested interests in the City and
the privatised monopolies in order to ensure their future profits, it was
dropped.

Table 2

Company name	Year	Total costs of sale to Her Majesty's Government including VAT, excluding incentives (£ thousands)
British Aerospace	1981	5,600
Cable and Wireless, 1981 sale	1981	8,900
Amersham International	1982	2,900
Britoil	1982	12,600
National Freight Corporation	1982	300
Associated British Ports	1983	2,600
British Petroleum, 1983 sale	1983	22,760
Cable and Wireless, 1983 sale	1983	12,500
Associated British Ports	1984	1,400
Enterprise Oil	1984	10,700
Jaguar	1984	n/a
Sealink	1984	100
Wytch Farm	1984	98
British Telecom	1984	183,000
British Aerospace	1985	17,800
Britoil	1985	23,300
Cable and Wireless, 1985 sale	1985	21,400
British Gas	1986	175,000
British Shipbuilding warship yards	1986	55,500
British Airways	1987	33,900
Rolls Royce	1987	41,600
Plant Breeding Institute	1987	822
Royal Ordnance	1987	1,900
BAA	1987	45,200
Rover Group	1987	1,800
British Petroleum, 1987 sale	1987	48,299
		730,861

In the light of these developments it is hardly surprising that the main
beneficiaries of privatisation have been the City institutions which

organised the sales and the top executives who now run the privatised companies. The former did very well indeed, and must rank as those who have done best out of the Thatcher years. For each flotation organised by a merchant bank, with back-up prospectuses from solicitors and reporting accountants, with advertising and public relations campaigns, with the huge underwriting commitments involved, costs have been enormous and far beyond the incentives individual shareholders have gained.

The flotation of British Gas alone cost £360 million, the expenses and incentives being nearly 5% of the proceeds. In the case of British Telecom and British Airports costs amounted to nearly 7% of the proceeds. For British Gas advertising alone cost £21 million. Advertising costs for all flotations so far have been £70 million, a massive budget which has gone to only a few firms.

As this table shows, more than £700 million has already been spent in selling off Britain's public assets, and another £1,000 million — a sum equivalent to 1p in the £ in income tax — is likely to be spent when electricity, water, British Coal, British Rail and what remains of British Telecom are successively sold off. Merchant banks and advertising agencies, among others, will benefit accordingly.

Top executives have done well too, compensating themselves for the additional responsibilities of life in the private sector with remarkable generosity. British Telecom's chairman was paid £153,000 a year in 1987, rising to £226,000 in 1988. When its first chairman after privatisation, Sir George Jefferson retired he accepted a pension and compensation package of £900,000, and he was not alone. The tables below show how top management salaries have moved since privatisation. The average rise in the first year was 78%.

And what about the workers? They have done less well. No dramatic pay rises for them, and not much pride of ownership either. According to an optimistic Treasury survey only 3% of the shares are held by the workforces of privatised companies.

Privatisation has happened and is likely to continue. Huge sums of money have changed hands and there is more, much more to come. The total value of the sales of public corporations and of public holdings in private companies amounts to £18 billion so far. Further sales could raise another £20 billion. But what does the balance sheet really mean for the nation and its citizens as taxpayers and consumers?

WHERE THERE IS GREED . . .

Table 3   Change in top executive salary in first year
after privatisation

	% increase
Cable & Wireless	114
Amersham	61
Britoil	23
Associated British Ports	23
Enterprise Oil	167
Jaguar	100
British Telecom	32
British Gas	68
British Airways	126
Rolls Royce	31
BAA	110
average	**78**

Directors have done well too.

Table 4

	Director remuneration (1988 prices)		Top executive remuneration (1988 prices)	
	1979 £	1988 £	1979 £	1988 £
Amersham	29,000	64,000	31,000	90,000
Associated British Ports	n/a	50,000	n/a	97,000
BAA	28,000	86,000	37,000	151,000
British Airways	35,000	142,000	45,000	253,000
British Gas	33,000	96,000	49,000	184,000
British Telecom	n/a	112,000	n/a	198,000
Britoil	n/a	n/a	n/a	n/a
Cable & Wireless	29,000	115,000	31,000	208,000
Enterprise Oil	n/a	87,000	n/a	135,000
Jaguar	n/a	96,000	n/a	218,000
National Freight Consortium	24,000	71,000	44,000	143,000
Rolls Royce	55,000	80,000	95,000	130,000
average privatised	**33,300**	**90,800**	**47,400**	**164,300**

The most comprehensive study so far shows that productivity changes in Britain appear to be wholly unrelated to privatisation. Productivity gains in industries like electricity and coal, which are still in the public sector, have been far greater than gains in the private or privatised sector. Future prospects for productivity depend on investment, not least in new technologies, but, according to one survey, research and development in the privatised sector has taken second place to short-term profits. British Telecom, for example, spent 2.6% of its turnover on R & D in 1984, but by 1988 the figure had fallen to 1.9%.

Crude Tory rhetoric apart, there is little evidence to justify the automatic benefits of privatisation. As one study has suggested, privatisation fails to address 'the more difficult areas where the market failure is by no means trivial . . . monopoly, public good and information'. There is, its authors say, 'tension between the failure of markets and the failure of regulation and the need to find structures which minimise the extent of either. This is a more complicated exercise than chanting slogans about the virtues of private enterprise.'

The warnings are as true of privatised services as they are of privatised industries. The record in local government and in the NHS of contracting out is one of lost jobs, deteriorating working conditions and in many cases falling standards of service. Detailed information is now beginning to come forward, such as an audit of the record of contracted-out local authority services in Manchester that revealed 'some of those companies which won contracts for school dinners . . . were providing underweight meals with insufficient nutritional value, under-cooked food and a lack of fresh vegetables; and not surprisingly there is a drop in the numbers of people wanting to eat such poor quality food'.

The goal of competition has been abandoned, productivity is lagging and consumers are unimpressed, yet there is no declared limit to the government's privatisation plans. One government minister has sug-gested that the boundary between private and public sector should be redefined so that only defence, law and order and some basic regulatory tasks might escape privatisation. 'Grey areas' where the private sector would become increasingly involved included, in his view, health and education, and already such developments are taking place.

Already firmly on the agenda are coal, rail transport, much of the Post Office, the work of many government departments, many local government services and, of course, water and electricity. In the light of commonsense and experience the water and electricity privatisations defy logic. Water privatisation may be proceeding simply because it is an obsession of the Prime Minister. From the point of view of the consumer water can never be anything but a total monopoly, and it is also a vital service in relation to public health.

The water assets which the government is now proposing to sell were

never bought by the government but were transferred from the ownership of the local authorities; 85% of people are against the sale. Twenty
million houses will have to be metered at a cost of £1.5 billion, a cost that
will be passed on to the consumer outside the regulatory structure.

Dividends after privatisation are estimated at £400 million. Once
again the consumer will pay. Water price rises of up to 30% — a figure
which Mr Ridley once said should be taken with a pinch of salt — are
only a start. Prices are more likely to double. The proposed regulatory
system will, almost certainly, lack the resources to monitor the privatised
system. There is talk of increased investment in water, something that
compliance with EEC directives now requires, yet the cost of cleaning up
our water supplies will be paid not by the polluter but by the consumer.

In the case of electricity, there is little real competition and none at the
point at which the consumer buys. To make electricity more attractive
for the City, Labour proposals to promote energy conservation have been
resisted. To reassure investors a nuclear levy will be charged to power
stations burning coal, oil or gas so that nuclear power stations, with costs
around 40% more than those using fossil fuels, will remain competitive.

This nuclear tax will probably cost each domestic consumer £20 a
year. And on top of that the government is expected to indemnify
investors against unforeseen escalations in nuclear costs, such as those
arising from closing power stations and disposing of nuclear waste.
Consumer interests have been subordinated to privatisation prospects,
and it is estimated that as a result consumers will be paying 25% more
for their electricity by 1990.

Privatisation has been a costly experiment whose benefits have been
at best dubious. It has cost £700 million in City fees alone, with £70
million of that going on marketing and advertising. Undervaluation of
assets has been enormous and culpable, an estimated £2,500 million
altogether. In the next round similar sums will be lost.

The losers have been the taxpayers, the winners undoubtedly the big
institutions in the City and top management of the privatised companies. There is no evidence that productivity has gone up, or that
consumers have benefited. The original pretext, that of consumer
advantage through competition-induced efficiency, has died quietly as
concerns have been privatised as monopolies. Despite all the rhetoric of
a battle by ministers against state corporations in the interests of consumers, the net result is a sell-out to the City, consumers all forgotten.

9

The Tories and the Polluters

'From our work on environmental issues over a number of years, we sense a growing concern . . . for consistent, effective, and scientifically justified environmental protection against every separate source of danger. We consider that the Department of the Environment has failed to provide the leadership and the commitment necessary to achieve this . . . never, in any of our enquiries into environmental problems, have we experienced such consistent and universal criticism of existing legislation and of central and local government as we have during the course of this enquiry . . . after a long and exhaustive enquiry we feel we must warn the government that by continuing to ignore previous recommendations it is playing — sometimes literally — with fire.'

All party select committee on the environment.
Second report on toxic waste, 22 February 1989

'No generation has a freehold on this earth, all we have is a life tenancy with a full repairing lease. This government intends to meet the terms of that lease in full.'

Mrs Thatcher, Conservative Party Conference, 14 October 1988

Of all Mrs Thatcher's initiatives over the last ten years none has received more publicity than her conversion to the cause of the environment. In a carefully crafted speech to the Royal Society, and later, in a Conservative Conference address, she sought to defuse public criticism of government environment policy and seize the political initiative on these issues from other parties. The conversion, however, was sudden and late and the real issues are still how much the environment has been neglected over the last ten years and how little her policies will do to prevent the same neglect from extending well into the Nineties.

WHERE THERE IS GREED ...

The key elements in Mrs Thatcher's environmental policies remain her reluctance to legislate, her faith in voluntary agreements and her support for what industry calls 'best practice'. All reflect the traditional Tory obeisance to vested interests and it is they, whether country landowners, industrial polluters or transport interests, who dominate the environment debate.

Margaret Thatcher does not believe in the polluter pays principle; but rather, as is transparently clear in the case of water, that the consumer pays to clear up the mess created by the polluter. Her latest phrase for the environment, 'Best Available Technology Not Entailing Excessive Cost' (BATNEEC), is merely a code for letting polluters get away with doing what they want.

Despite being forced into the 1986 Food and Environment Protection Act, the introduction of Environmentally Sensitive Areas and the setting up of Her Majesty's Pollution Inspectorate, the government has done little to address the environmental problems Britain faces. Up to 11 million Britons live in areas supplied with water that does not meet EEC standards. Water pollution incidents have risen in number from 12,500 in 1980 to 23,253 in 1987. River pollution, caused by slurry and silage effluent from farms, rose to an all-time high with more than 4,000 cases in 1988. Our beaches are the dirtiest in Europe. At least one-third of them fail the standards required by the EEC Bathing Water Directive.

In the dumping of waste in the North Sea Britain is the worst offender and Britain has become the waste disposal centre of Europe. Every year Britain produces 2 million tons of airborne sulphur and is the most copious emitter of sulphur dioxide in Western Europe. Fewer than 1% of our cars use unleaded petrol and last year in Britain 3,000 tons of lead were pumped into the air. The government has cut the budget for the Energy Efficiency Office, ridden roughshod over local planning controls and cut local authority budgets for dealing with waste litter and toxic hazards.

Behind the public relations, advertising slogans and juvenile jingles about litter there is a covert theme: the shifting of blame. The government is not responsible. The free market is blameless. When it can no longer be denied that things have gone wrong blame will be attached to an individual, to a lapse from 'standard practice', to a foreign government or to the failings of a past Labour government.

And in tackling any problem certain ground rules apply. There must be no increase in public spending and any threat to future privatisation plans must be avoided. More importantly, the business interests to which the Conservative Party is so beholden must not be damaged or even offended. And when action can no longer be avoided the programme proposed enjoys a ten-year timescale that will place any test of its effectiveness well beyond the next election.

The government's true strategy is best summarised not by the polished statements of the Prime Minsiter but by the unedited remarks of the Environment Minister, Lord Caithness, as he spoke in the Lords of litter and noise: 'We must really get away from the idea that "they" ought to do something about it, and develop the idea that "we" can do something about it.' Referring to noise, and including presumably aircraft noise and factory noise, his injunction continued, 'as with litter it [noise] is a form of pollution that will only be solved by individual action. Local mess is created by us and it is up to us to sort it out.'

Concern for the environment is a very late addition to the Thatcher agenda. There were few concessions to the green lobby in the Conservative manifestoes of 1979 and 1983. Indeed the 1985 list of 'enemies within' included environmentalists. There has been little action on the environment and the story has mainly been one of delay and obstruction to the initiatives of others. When in 1983 the Brundtland Commission on Environmental Development was set up, to report in 1987, the British government hardly even paid lipservice to it.

According to Stanley Clinton Davies, the EEC Commissioner most concerned with environmental issues, the Prime Minister's Royal Society speech of October 1988 was notable for being 'the first time in living memory that Mrs Thatcher allowed the word environment to escape from her lips'. 'The trouble is,' Davies writes, 'that for nearly four years as European Commissioner I have seen first-hand evidence of the government in action, or rather inaction, on the Community stage on nearly all the issues so carefully selected by the Prime Minister. There they were, I suppose they would say leading from the rear, obstructing, objecting to proposals to reduce atmospheric pollution, water pollution, to improve the quality of human and animal life. Any excuse to avoid or delay progress would be deployed: "More research ... more studies are needed", "The scientific case has not been fully established ... Industry is not ready", "Market forces must be allowed to set the pace" and of course, "It impairs national sovereignty".'

It was in fact under a Labour administration that the Control of Pollution Act was passed some 20 years ago, and the establishment of the Royal Commission on Environmental Pollution even before that first recognised and tackled pollution as a threat not just to public health but also to the environment and the quality of life. The Tory approach is different. Mrs Thatcher's main response has been to keep government out of it and rely as far as possible on leaving environmental issues to the operation of market forces. While at one point the Prime Minister was forced to concede that it is 'the government's job to set standards and no one else can do it', the free market, in practice the business interests that dominate it, has dictated the course of events for ten years. No attempt has been made to force the polluter to pay, or to introduce the 'precautionary principle', whereby the potential polluter has to prove that the discharge for which he is responsible does not pose a risk to the environment.

The Tory approach to the protection of landscape and wildlife has also been weak and singularly undemanding for the relevant interest groups. The 1981 Wildlife and Countryside Act, forced upon the government by the EEC Rare Birds Directive, is the main legislation involved. In practice it became a convenient mechanism by which the government managed to subsidise already wealthy landowners. Protection for wildlife sites is guaranteed by means of compensation for their owners. Thus Lord Thurso received £287,000 for a 99-year lease on an area that had previously been declared a National Nature Reserve. Lord Cranbourne must be equally grateful for an index-linked £20,000 a year for maintaining one of the finest woods in southern England. Farmers all over the country are being paid handsomely for doing what they should be doing anyway.

The protection of natural waterways of scenic and natural history importance has probably been weakened by the new Broads Act, whereby any overriding duty of conservation has been removed, a change that will favour commercial interests. Private Members' Bills to protect hedgerows and extend Tree Preservation Orders to locally important hedgerows have been blocked. Ministers have failed to close a loophole in the Act which allows species to be killed as an incidental result of lawful felling. They have also failed to provide statutory protection for sites of special scientific interest or provide effective legislation for the establishment of marine nature reserves. No attempt has been made to give local authorities power to make landscape conservation orders that could be enforced without compensation. In general, planning controls have been reduced in line with the government's policy of not interfering with the workings of market forces. As the White Paper *Lifting the Burden* made clear in 1986, planning control 'imposes costs on the economy and constraints on enterprise that are not always justified by any real public benefit in the individual case'. It is privatisation, not regulation, that the government favours, as can be seen from the 1988 proposal to hand over to the private sector up to one-third of the National Nature Reserves, and from the 1989 plan to allow the sale of land currently in the hands of the water authorities.

The disposal of waste is now a major problem. In Britain today 90% of our waste is consigned to landfill sites. In Germany only 70% of waste is so managed, in France 35% and in Denmark 30%. The method is undesirable and sometimes unsafe. In January 1989 Mrs Bottomley, the Environment Minister, had to admit that 1,400 rubbish tips contained dangerous quantities of explosive methane gas and that only one-third of all tips had any form of gas control. The Liverpool Garden Festival site has now had to be closed because of a build-up of methane in the rubbish dump on which it was built. Little progress has been made towards increasing the number — only 35 at present — of municipal incinerators, which burn rubbish and could also, as happens in Lausanne in Switzerland, generate usable thermal energy for heating or industrial purposes.

There has been little effort in Britain to recycle waste, despite public support for the concept and evidence that up to 80% could be recycled if only facilities existed. Britain stands at 11th out of 12 in the European recycling league, for example managing to recycle only 13% of glass used for containers. In Germany households are issued with two kinds of rubbish bin, one for recyclable, one for non-recyclable waste, and in ten American states there is now mandatory recycling. Here in the UK we have as yet neither legislation to encourage industries to provide recycling facilities nor tax incentives to make reclamation more attractive. As a result there is little effort by industry to utilise packaging materials suitable for recycling or to make packaging returnable.

A recent survey suggested that more than 70% of households would use bottle banks but at present there are only 2,500 of them — one for every 14,000 people, compared to one for every 1,000–2,000 in almost all major European countries. Only 2% of the millions of cans used each year are recycled. Less than 20% of our newspapers are recycled and most of our glass — around 85% — is used only once. The evidence is that the squeeze on local authority funding has compelled cutbacks on glass recycling and waste paper collection schemes. Once again the government has withheld public money, discussed voluntary measures and fastidiously refrained from anything that might look like putting pressure on business interests. Wastefully, we continue to bury much recyclable waste.

With toxic wastes the stakes are higher: public safety rather than economy. The disposal of toxic waste is a great and immediate problem, with 1.6 million tonnes of hazardous waste building up every year in Britain for disposal, somehow. Just how is a matter of increasing uncertainty and growing public concern. The provisions of the Control of Pollution Act of 1974, which required that all disposal operations for controlled waste be licensed, were considerably weakened by new regulations in 1980 and urgently require reinforcement by means of legislation which will place the onus of safety firmly on the potential polluter.

The hazards created by the disposal of toxic waste are widespread and in many cases alarmingly indeterminate. With only five waste inspectors to supervise 5,600 dumps in England and Wales alone, the government does not even have a complete inventory of abandoned dumps. Its own Hazardous Wastes Inspectorate is concerned that 83% of hazardous waste is going into landfill sites, with only 9% disposed of by incineration or by chemical treatment. Repeated criticism by the Hazardous Waste Inspectorate has had little effect.

Given the risks and the level of public concern about the matter, the feebleness of the government in facing the commercial interests concerned is culpable. It appears reluctant even to cause offence, and the current law is so weak that when Britain's biggest waste treatment group, Leigh Interests, was found guilty on 12 charges brought under provisions of the Control of Pollution Act it was fined only £7,000. Joan Ruddock's new backbench Bill seeks to prevent illegal waste dumping by registering carriers but the government resists her proposal to enforce penalties by the impounding of vehicles. The government alternative? A 'duty to care'.

By such demonstrations of laxity the government has in effect declared Great Britain the dustbin of Europe. Imports of waste are booming, with 'special waste' rising from 3,786 tonnes in 1981 to an estimated 180,000 tonnes in 1988. Feeble controls make for lower costs, and it is a measure of the risks to our population that the disposal costs that triggered this unwelcome boom are a third of those in Belgium and a fifth of those in France and Germany. Waste is now coming into Britain from Holland, Portugal, Belgium, West Germany, Denmark, Norway, Sweden, Spain, Italy, Switzerland and even from America, Canada, Hong Kong, Australia and Singapore.

In 1981 the government was urged by a House of Lords Select Committee that 'a new sense of urgency' be brought to bear on the problem. Attention has yet to be given to the problems of landfill gas hazards and groundwater pollution. There has been no serious action on alternative treatment technologies.

Recent events have shown how reluctant the government is to do anything. Last summer the Nigerian government found 3,800 tonnes of poisonous waste that had been illegally imported from Italy. When the ship *Karin B*, with 2,000 tonnes of that waste on board, headed for Britain, the British government was forced, in its fashion, to act. While the ship could be refused a landing, the government had no proper powers to deal with the problem because of its failure to implement the 1986 EEC directive on the transfrontier shipment of toxic waste. An embarrassing 22 months after the expiry of the deadline for implementation the government rushed into action.

Only stopgap legislation resulted. Strong and comprehensive measures to ban shipments of hazardous waste, end the dumping at sea of industrial waste and ensure that the Pollution Inspectorate has adequate powers to control all pollution are still awaited. Meanwhile, the government continues to resist public and professional pressure. In November 1988 the government's Chief Inspector of Pollution — in charge of monitoring air, water and toxic waste pollution — resigned and senior inspectors claimed the government was refusing to support the Inspectorate. Earlier a deputy, Mr David Mills, who resigned as Chief Inspector of Hazardous Waste, had drawn attention to the government's failure to enforce existing controls. One document showed that the annual total of inspections by air inspectors had gone down from 11,000 to 8,000 over a period of three years.

The government's response — to appoint an additional 13 pollution inspectors and to raise hopes about a Waste Management Bill currently inching forward in the parliamentary queue — is generally regarded as inadequate. And despite the May 1988 regulations, extending the scope of waste disposal licensing and collection systems, and the February 1989 proposals to separate the regulatory and operational functions of the English and Welsh waste disposal authorities, Britain is still waiting for new laws backed up by adequate arrangements for their enforcement. The matter is all the more pressing since numbers of licensed sites are expected to rise to around 15,000 over the coming years.

As Clinton Davies has said, 'On issues fundamental to the health of our people they have so frequently failed to honour directives, laws, to which they themselves have subscribed their names, albeit grudgingly . . . They caused Britain to gain the offensive reputation of the dirty man of Europe.' Whether by their rejection of most of the recommendations of the Royal Commission on Environmental Pollution Report or by their continued failure to ensure proper regulation government ministers have shown themselves incapable of acting in the public interest for fear of offending commercial interests that to them seem to matter more.

They have failed also in the control of air pollution. Lead added to our atmosphere each year totals 3,000 tonnes as a result of the increasing use of petrol, only a fraction of which is at present unleaded. Despite the knowledge that lead damages the health of children, affecting particularly their intellectual development, ministers have been slow to encourage the use of unleaded petrol, widening the price differential with leaded significantly only in the budget of April 1989. Lack of government encouragement has been an important factor in the poor availability of unleaded petrol, with only 11% of stations in England and Wales and 12% of those in Scotland stocking it. Yet by 1990 the UK must obey an EEC directive that all new cars must be capable of running on lead-free petrol.

The government's record on the control of industrial air pollution has been dismal. Only after the European Commission threatened legal action against the UK's persistent failure to install modern pollution control equipment did the government drop its long-standing objection to an EEC directive designed to curb sulphur dioxide and nitrogen oxide emissions from large combustion plants. Even then only one of our 40 fossil-fuelled power stations will be cleaned up during the current government term. Britain's vehicle emission standards are also lax and it was Britain's obstructive attitude that compelled a weak EEC agreement on the subject.

The British government has also refused to take the necessary action on a number of threats to the upper atmosphere. Increased energy efficiency, leading to diminished carbon dioxide production from fossil fuels, would help, but UK government action on this lags behind. More could be done to speed the eventual abandonment of the use of CFCs. Although several European governments have pledged to reduce their nitrogen oxide emissions by 30% the UK is not one of them. 40% of nitrogen oxides come from motor vehicles and the government has chosen to accommodate the motor manufacturers rather than adopt the tighter US standards which have been in place since 1983. Once more industrial interests have prevailed.

The technology is available. Catalytic converters were introduced in America and Japan in the mid-Seventies and are now mandatory in countries like Austria, Switzerland, Sweden and Canada. There are even tax incentives to help West Germans decide on environmentally cleaner cars. But for commercial reasons the UK motor industry has opted only for lean burn engines, a less effective means of limiting emissions, and the government has come up with the desired resistance to EEC regulatory efforts.

Attempts in Britain to control chemical threats to the ozone layer have been characterised by a lack of enthusiasm and the customary deference to the sectarian interests of the industry. Damaging aerosol propellants could and should have been phased out ten years ago. In the international discussion that finally resulted in the Montreal agreement of 1987 the UK government acted as lobbyist for an industry reluctant to change. Even the labelling of aerosol cans, so that consumers could make an informed choice and perhaps eventually trigger change, was not brought in. The US government did far better, banning CFCs as propellants in 1978.

The consequences for trees of acid rain, caused by emissions of huge amounts of nitrogen oxide and sulphur dioxide, are well known.

Perhaps less well known is the finding of a UN report that 57% of British conifers have been seriously damaged, a figure that is the highest in Europe. The explanation is obvious and local to these islands: large plant emissions of sulphur dioxide in the UK now amount to 3.3 million tonnes a year. Our trees will continue to be the sickest in Europe because of the government's attitudes to European attempts to enforce controls. Britain has fought against all measures aimed at reducing power station emissions, has secured lengthy delays and has now engineered a deal with Europe that allows a reduction of only 9% on today's sulphur dioxide output. Legislation for scrubbers on power stations has also been resisted.

While it is official policy to maintain and improve the quality of Britain's water, in practice little has been done. Since 1979 the quality of our rivers has steadily declined. Large stretches of top quality rivers, previously classed as 1A and 1B, have deteriorated over the Eighties. Expenditure of several billions will be required to improve sewage treatment, to control sewage discharges and to meet existing and future standards. There are at present only very inadequate controls over the use of agrochemicals including pesticides and nitrate-based fertilisers — one of the principle reasons for the recent fight with the EEC over the drinking water directive.

Water pollution incidents from farm slurry and silage effluent are now the highest ever, reaching a record 4,000 in 1988 and forcing the Agricultural Minister to complain of 'recklessness'. While industrial waste is the major source of pollution — 37% of all incidents — farm waste is now responsible for nearly 20% of incidents. As the report, *Water Pollution from Farm Waste*, states, 'undiluted farm slurry is ... up to 100 times more polluting than untreated sewage. Silage liquor is even stronger at 200 times.' Yet the maximum fine for such pollution is only £2,000 and the average fine levied only £330. Threats to water supplies also come from the coal tar linings of our water pipes and the use of aluminium in water treatment.

The government itself has aggravated the problem of sewage contamination by relaxing the standards for discharges allowed from at least 1,800 of the 6,000 sewage treatment plants in England and Wales. The prosecution of water-polluting offenders is at best desultory. For example, less than 2% of reported incidents of water pollution in 1987 resulted in prosecution. The number of incidents is rising steadily, with more than 23,000 in 1988, twice the figure for 1980.

Where generally there should have been moves towards energy saving, the government has done little. Energy conservation could save up to £7 billion in fuel bills. Department of Energy officials have even calculated that the widespread application of up-to-date technologies could cut the demand for electricity by as much as 40%. The Tory response to this challenge has been to cut the budget of the Energy Efficiency Office from £26 million in 1987–88 to £20 million last year and only £10 million by 1990–91. TV advertising campaigns on energy savings have been switched off. There has been no serious attempt to explore a transition to less polluting sources of energy and support for research into renewable sources such as solar energy and wave power has been reduced.

Grants under the Home Insulation Scheme have fallen by 25% over ten years. In 1979 energy conservation work was completed on 632,000 dwellings. In 1987 the figure was just over a tenth of that, 67,000. Worst of all no obligation is to be placed on the privatised electricity industry to conserve as well as to produce. Its energy policy will be one of sell, sell, sell, because when the government faces a choice between imposing regulation on privatised industry and allowing market forces to operate unrestrained there is never any doubt about the outcome.

The position of the oil industry seems to be particularly strong. The government has failed to impose any depletion policy on its exploitation of North Sea resources. The industry's power over environmental interests has been dramatically demonstrated in Dorset. When Wytch Field was extended to allow oil drilling in Poole harbour, Dorset's Chief Planning Officer was driven to note that, 'If oil development is allowed in an area which is a site of Special Scientific Interest, an area of Outstanding Natural Beauty and part of a Heritage Coast, there are few areas where it can be legitimately refused.'

This overall neglect of our environment will continue well into the Nineties. Despite Mrs Thatcher's claims that there has been increased support for environmental research, spending by the Department of the Environment fell in value from £41 million in 1979 to £29 million last year, with resultant cuts in research into radioactive waste, air pollution, toxic substances and the countryside. Total government spending, already miserly at £1 for every £6 that the West German government spends on the same problems, will fall further in value over the next three years. As the Chair of the National Environment Research Council concedes, staff have had to be cut, capital expenditure curtailed and grants for university research reduced. Yet such is the sway of privatisation and the commercial lobby that some of this scarce public money is actually being diverted to 'support trials of water metering'.

In ten years there have been no new resources and few new ideas. As a substitute for genuine policy there has been a public relations initiative. Public expenditure has been curtailed and the appeasement of vested interests extended. When government ministers say that 'solutions are for industry' and duck the only effective option, that of making the polluter pay, it becomes clear just where the power lies. A government that relies on market forces to solve environmental problems is one that is supine before vested interests and culpably negligent of its responsibilities.

A less likely guarantee of a healthy environment is hard to imagine. 'Leave companies alone and they will regard water and air as free dumping grounds,' warns no less an authority than the impeccably right-wing *Economist*. 'Without government help the market cannot say useful things about disposing of waste . . . It is for government on behalf of voters to decide how clean they want the world to be. Markets cannot decide that for them.'

10

Unequal Britain: How the Rich Became Richer

'Neither is it necessary to allay any general feelings of injustice in society.'

Mrs Thatcher, 1975

'Does the budget mark the end of the use of taxation to redistribute wealth in this country?'
Nigel Lawson: 'I hope so. I hope we are in a new era in this country.'

1988

The distribution of income in Britain has now become so unequal that it is beginning to resemble that of a Third World country. Since 1979 an extraordinary transfer of resources, from poor to rich, has taken place. The outstanding characteristic of the oil years since 1979 has not been the diffusion of oil wealth to us all, but the growing affluence of the few at the expense of the very poor. Most of us, despite ten years of rhetoric about tax cutting, are actually paying more tax, but for the few at the top the rhetoric means something, in many cases a great deal. The richer you are, the more your taxes have been cut.

Since 1979 income and wealth inequalities have grown at a faster rate than at any time since the war. Over the Fifties, Sixties and Seventies the share of national income enjoyed by the richest tenth of the population fell from about one-third to just over one-quarter. The share of the top 1% fell from 11% to just over 5%. Proceeding more slowly than most other developed countries, Britain was at least on its way to becoming a fairer society.

Over the years since Mrs Thatcher came to power all that has changed. By 1985 the top 10% had recovered all the ground they had lost in the previous 20 years, and for half the population, the bottom 50%, their share of the national income had fallen to its lowest point since 1945. As Thomas Stark, an authority on these themes, has observed, 'It appears that the trend to equality has halted'.

Upper income Britain is doing very nicely. The position of the top 1% and the top 10% makes for illuminating reading. The top 10% had seen their pre-tax income fall to 24% by 1979. By 1985 it had risen to 29% at the expense of those further down the scale. The distribution of income after tax reveals the same trend. The top 10% had 23% and, by 1985, 26.5%. The top 1% have done even better, their post-tax income rising from 4% in 1979 to 5% in 1985.

Table 1 Income distribution before and after tax

	1979		1984–85	
	Pre-tax	Post-tax	Pre-tax	Post-tax
Top 1%	5%	3.9%	6.4%	4.9%
Top 5%	16%	10%	18.5%	16%
Top 10%	26.1%	23.4%	29.5%	26.5%
Bottom 20%	5.9%	7.0%	5.8%	6.9%

It is possible to gauge the trends in income distribution after 1985, by looking at taxpayers, and not the population as a whole. Once again the trend is very clear. In 1989 the top 1% of taxpayers had 6% of income after tax, twice what they had in 1979.

Table 2 Distribution of income only among taxpayers
Before Tax and After Tax

	Pre-tax	Post-tax
1978–79		
Top 1%	5%	3%
Top 5%	15%	10%
Top 10%	24%	21%
Bottom 25%	11%	13%
1988–89		
Top 1%	7%	6%
Top 5%	17%	15%
Top 10%	27%	25%
Bottom 25%	9%	11%

As we move out of the 1980s the tiniest but richest fraction of the population, the 200,000 who form the top 1% of taxpayers, have been the decade's biggest beneficiaries by far. As we shall see below, the bottom 20%, 4 million households, have done particularly badly as a result and have become worse off not only in relative but in absolute terms. The yuppification of society, in which Mrs Thatcher would have us believe, has simply not taken place. Indeed it would be difficult to argue that there remains even a common interest between that top 1%, to whom Mrs Thatcher has given so much, and the rest of the nation.

This growing inequality has not been evident in Europe as a whole. While all countries have seen more women at work, a growing elderly population and more unemployment, all of which tend to increase inequalities between household incomes, no country has seen such a growth in inequality as ours because none has witnessed such a withdrawal by the state from wage protection and social security, or experienced such a growth in regressive taxation.

A report from the European Commission on *Trends and Distribution of Incomes: an Overview* makes it clear that 'in France and Germany there was a significant decrease in income inequality, in Spain and Italy a substantial stability and in the UK an increasing disparity'. In brief summary, 'after 1979, with the Conservative government in charge, labour market relations were more than before left to the play of demand and supply. This resulted in a further rise in unemployment and in a widening of wage differentials. The commitment of the government to limit the role of the state was implemented through, among other things, cuts in social expenditure and regressive changes in the system of taxation. The obvious result was an increase in inequality, not only in original income distribution but in gross income and disposable income as well.'

Wealth is far more unequally distributed than income. The evidence is that the top 10% now own more than 50% of all wealth, while the bottom 50% own only 7%. In cash terms the wealth of the top 1%, who now own 17%, has more than doubled under the Conservatives. In real terms the rises are also impressive. On average the real value of the wealth of individuals in the top 1% has increased from £380,000 to an estimated £572,000 between 1979 and 1989, making their average stake more than half a million pounds. For the top 2% the rise is equally impressive. Their average individual share has risen by £130,000 to an estimated £404,000.

Table 3   Average wealth per head
[Marketable wealth of individuals]

£. 1989 prices		1979	1989	Real increase	Share of total
Top	1%	380,000	572,000	193,000	17%
Bottom	50%	3,130	4,710	1,590	7%
Top	2%	268,000	404,000	136,000	24%

It goes on. The top 1% own 64% of all land, 53% of company shares as well as 17% of net wealth. The richest 5% own 80% of shares and 86% of land. In the eight years from 1976 to 1984, the most recent period for which figures are available, the ownership of land has become even more concentrated. The richest 1% have increased their holdings by 12% from 52% over these eight years.

The occupational pattern of wealth holders at the top has changed too, with fewer industrialists and exporters, more salesmen, financiers, property developers and retailers. And although only five aristocratic families now make it into the top 20 of Britain's richest, 100 of the top 200 familes that have assets worth more than £10 million inherited their money.

Retailing is the foundation of much of the new wealth, with property second. There are 53 retailers and 31 property developers in the top 200. Whatever it is, owning these businesses is strongly recommended. The City is another major source of new wealth, thanks to golden hellos, golden handshakes, golden handcuffs and the celebrated telephone number salaries, but increasingly absent from the list of the richest are industrialists and manufacturers. With notable exceptions — like Mr Alan Sugar who imports most of his Amstrad products — there have been few equivalents for the 1980s of the Nuffields, the Cadburys, the Rowntrees, the Courtaulds and the Leverhulmes.

In 1986, in a section of a speech she was due to deliver but which she removed at the last moment, Mrs Thatcher wrote of her vision of 'a society in which the British family would be worth £100,000'. If that is indeed her aim, its achievement is a long way off. Even if the family home is thrown in, the vast majority of families — 93% in total — have far less than £100,000 and are far from obtaining such a sum. The wealth that the majority of the population — the poorest 50% — owns averages only £6,900 if occupational pensions are included and £4,700 if they are not.

The importance of Mrs Thatcher's stated aim is not whether or not it can be achieved, but how it betrays a view of society that excludes the great majority of the averagely or less well off. The concept of inequality in society must be very difficult to find important if the concept of society is so limited in the first place. Perhaps the inequality she has created is to her not so much unthinkable as merely unnoticed.

But inequality there is, and an understanding of how it was created depends on the consideration of two aspects of government policy: the widening of wage differentials and the increasingly regressive nature of taxation.

For those at the top pre-tax pay has increased substantially since 1979. Today there are 17,000 who earn more than £100,000 yearly and 110,000 who earn more than £50,000. In 1979 the best off tenth received on average incomes six times those of the worst off tenth. By 1985 the top tenth was receiving nearly ten times as much. In real terms the salaries of top executives and top directors have doubled over ten years. The average private sector senior executive salary is now £134,000, the average director's remuneration now £213,000, again up 90% in real terms since 1979. The very people who spend much of their energies calling for wage restraint have been awarding themselves very large increases indeed. Up there perks are valuable too. A 1987 survey found that 20% of the average remuneration of managing directors was paid in the form of perks. 50% received bonuses as a matter of course, received help with lunches and phone bills, and more than 70% had share options and free medical insurance. Most enjoyed company cars, still a valuable perk. Profit-related pay deals have, on average, increased earnings at the top by 10%.

Even if the value of perks is discounted there has been a substantial increase in living standards at the top. For the top 10% the salary increase, after taking inflation into account, is 31%. For the top 25% of earners it is 25%. For the bottom 10% the increase is only 8%. Indeed while the real value of earnings for professional and managerial

Table 4   Pre-tax annual pay

	1979	1988	Real change
10% earned more than	£13,816	£18,106	+31%
25% earned more than	£10,845	£13,572	+25%
50% earned more than	£8,460	£9,927	+17%
25% earned less than	£6,461	£7,259	+12%
10% earned less than	£5,155	£5,569	+8%

staff rose by 28% between 1979 and 1986, and for managers by 20.6%, the rise for assembly workers has been only 3%, for transport workers 4% and for construction workers only 2%.

As with all advanced countries, Britain's industrial and occupational structure has changed remarkably since 1979, as one type of industrial economy has been transformed into another. While the post-war industrial economy employed large numbers of skilled production workers, the new economy employs professional and technological workers at one extreme and waiters, secretaries, shop assistants, cashiers and unskilled labour at the other, creating a more polarised labour market with a greatly reduced proportion of jobs offering middle income standards of pay.

More women are in work, but they are more concentrated in part-time work and the least skilled work. In 1979, 24% of employed women were in unskilled and semi-skilled jobs. By 1985 the figure was 36%, and over that period the earnings gap between skilled and unskilled work has grown. Britain now has two sharply contrasted labour markets: a primary labour market with relatively good wages and job security, existing side by side with a secondary labour market made up of jobs that are less rewarding, in many cases temporary or part-time, and all low paid. For millions of families only the fact that both husband and wife are working has prevented them from falling even further behind.

Over the course of ten years Britain has become established as one of the low pay economies of Europe. Since 1979 the number of adults falling below the 'decency threshold' of the Council of Europe (two-thirds of median earnings, or £135 weekly) has grown from 38% of the workforce to 47%, from less than 7.8 million to 9.4 million. 6.2

million of these are women, more than half of them part-time. Over that same period pay rises for the best paid 20% of the workforce have been 50% greater than for the low paid. Indeed, in contrast with the rest of the workforce, the earnings potential of the poorest tenth is now no greater today, at 64% of the median wage, than it was a century ago, at 68% in 1886, and it has declined significantly in the last ten years.

Poverty and inequality are therefore being generated from the workplace. Wage rates are inadequate and as a result many millions of individuals have insufficient resources to cover periods of sickness or unemployment or to ensure a decent standard of living in old age.

In 1990 the Conservatives plan to abolish Wages Councils which, in 1979, covered 2.87 million workers and today cover 2.47 million, most of whom work in pubs and restaurants. Already the Fair Wages clause of 1897 has been removed, Wages Council agreements watered down and young people removed from their scope, as part of the Conservative drive to ensure that the 'Wages Councils do not reduce job opportunities by forcing workers to charge unrealistic wage rates or employers to offer them'.

These 'unrealistic' wage rates range from £1.96 an hour to £2.50 an hour for the two and a half million workers covered. In the rag trade an adult worker will earn no more than £77.54 for a 39-hour week, in pubs and bars only £83 or £2.16 an hour. These are the official figures. Since 1979, 88,174 companies have been found to be underpaying their workers, although only 56 of them have been prosecuted. The true number of firms underpaying is probably far greater than that quoted because over the last ten years the number of wage inspectors, who are responsible for enforcing the legislation, has been more than halved, from 177 to 71.

Whole areas of economic life lie outside national minimum wage standards. The tower blocks of London and the Midlands house around 40,000 women home-workers, some of them earning only 50p for sewing a skirt or 6p for packaging a dozen stockings. Small clothing companies, which have increased in numbers from 10,000 to 30,000 since 1980 in London alone and from 5,000 to 20,000 in the Midlands, pay as little as £1 an hour, with even many of the best-organised of them offering only £2.

Table 5 Numbers falling below the Council of Europe's decency threshold

	1979	1987
Full-time men	1,640	2,560
Full-time women	3,000	2,780
All full-time	4,640	5,350
Part-time men	170	650
Part-time women	2,990	3,430
Total	7,800	9,430
% workforce	38.1%	45.8%

Women in part-time work, black workers (where the gap with white workers has actually grown) and young people have suffered most. In 1979 teenagers over 18 earned around 60% of adult wages, but by 1987 only 54%. The whole philosophy of wage cuts for the weakest, alongside tax cuts for the wealthiest, has been laid bare by Professor Alan Walters, the Prime Minister's own economic adviser, who has described the purpose of the original Young Workers scheme as 'first and foremost to put pressure on nominal wages offered to young workers . . . perhaps to substitute some of this cheap labour for existing more expensive employment'. The Youth Training Scheme, he wrote, had 'the same underlying quality that it was designed to work with rather than against market forces'. The 'anachronism' of Wages Councils would come under pressure as a result. The whole aim was the 'adjustment of real wages'. No doubt, he has written, they would have 'proceeded faster' if alongside trade union legislation they had abolished Wages Councils earlier and restructured the tax and benefits system.

If increasing disparities in earnings have accounted for much of the growing inequality in Britain today, increasing unfairness in the tax system explains most of the rest of it. The major change in tax of the last ten years has not been the reduction of the burden but a redistribution of it so that the very rich pay a lot less. For low and middle income Britain the tax take has increased, for those at the very top, and for them only, it has declined.

When the Conservatives came to power in 1979 determined to cut taxes Britain was a country in the middle rank for taxation. Ten years later it is still a middle rank country, though the total tax take has increased from 34% of national income to 38%. Even after the reduction of all rates of income tax British starting rates are still among the highest in the world. Whereas in Switzerland that starting rate is 1%, France 5%, Japan 10%, Italy 12% and the USA 15%, the starting rate in Britain is 25%. And because of increases in National Insurance and in indirect taxes, both regressive in their impact, most people are paying more in total taxes than they were in 1979. Where change has taken place is in the reduction of the top rate, which is now just about the lowest of all our major competitors.

In 1979 a married couple on three-quarters of average earnings with no children paid 28.9% of their earnings in all taxes including VAT. By 1989 they are paying 32.0% of their income. A couple with two children who paid 27.3% of their income in taxes in 1979 is now paying 29.7% in 1989. The same picture emerges for someone on average earnings. In 1979 they were paying 33.1% of their income in all taxes. Today it is 35.3%. A couple on average earnings with two children was paying 32.1% in 1979 and 33.6% in 1989. Worst of all are couples on half

Table 6   All Taxes as a share of Income

	1979	1989
Couple on average earnings, both at work	28.9%	32.0%
Couple on 75% of average earnings, one at work, with two children	27.3%	29.7%
Couple on average earnings, both at work	33.1%	35.3%
Couple on average earnings, one at work, with two children	32.1%	33.6%

average earnings. They paid 16% of their income in Income tax and National Insurance in 1979 and pay 18.5% today.

The real beneficiaries of Tory tax reforms have been the few at the top of the scale. For the top 1% of taxpayers a number of measures were enacted which ensured that the really significant tax gains went to the tiny majority of the already wealthy. The investment income surcharge was abolished. The top rate was cut from 83% to 60% and then to 40%, so that Britain now has the lowest tax rate on high incomes of any country apart from Switzerland. And in the 1988 Budget alone the top 1% received £1,880 million in income tax cuts, £220 million in inheritance tax reductions and a further £150 million from changes in capital gains tax.

Over ten years the cumulative gain for the top 1% from income tax cuts alone has been £26.6 billion (while the bottom 10% have had to make do with only £900 million). The 200,000 individuals who make up the top 1% have had income tax reductions averaging £10,000 a year, making cumulative gains of £100,000 each during Mrs Thatcher's rule. That tiny but overprivileged group received 32% of the tax cuts in the 1988 budget and has been given 29% of the total tax cuts between 1979 and 1988. In the simplest terms, the top 1% have received a bigger share of tax cuts than the bottom 70%.

Table 7   Total income tax cuts since 1979

	Total 1978–89	Budget 1988	% share of cuts 1978–89	% share of cuts 1988–89
Top 1%	£26.2b	£1.9b	29%	32%
Top 5%	£40.9b	£2.7b	45%	45%
Top 10%	£50.2b	£3.1b	55%	52%
Bottom 70%	£22.8b	£1.7b	25%	28%
Bottom 50%	£11.4b	£1.0b	12%	17%
Bottom 30%	£4.1b	£0.5b	4%	8%
Bottom 10%	£0.9b	£0.1b	1%	2%
Total	£91.2b	£6.0b		

Not only income tax changes have favoured the very rich. Changes in capital and inheritance taxation have helped them too, making Britain's inequalities even greater. One line in the 1989 Finance Bill handed the Duke of Westminster (estimated wealth £3,200 million) another £600 million. Capital taxes are now less and are paid by far fewer people, with many of the richest able to avoid paying tax at all. In 1978–79 capital gains tax was paid by 225,000 taxpayers. Today it is paid by only 20,000. Ten years ago 11 estates valued at over £1 million, and 34 valued at over £10.5 million completely escaped inheritance tax. Today 53 over £1 million and 200 over £0.5 million manage it. In the 1988 Budget alone the total reduction in inheritance tax for the top 200 taxable estates averaged £250,000 per taxpayer. Thanks to such changes the richest

1 % have seen their unearned income rise by 346% in ten years, and by 89% in one year alone thanks to the 1988 Budget.

And as if all this were not enough the Chancellor has been generous in the deployment of new and lucrative tax shelters for the very rich whose taxes he has slashed over the years. These include provisions relating to Enterprise Zones in the inner cities and the use of the Business Expansion Scheme, a form of tax shelter which proved popular in the financing of private hospitals, private health clinics, private nursing homes and even private schools. The latest manifestation of this has been in the area of private rented accommodation, a characteristic wonder of the Thatcher era, in effect a tax shelter that allows the rich to become richer by means of a partial and inefficient privatised response to the cutback in housing and social services for the poor.

It is now possible for someone earning £1 million to pay no income tax at all. The theory behind these tax allowances is that capital will flourish, that industry and innovation will thereby profit and enterprise be justly rewarded. The realities are more mundane and more squalid. The rewards are for ingenuity in tax avoidance only. The economy as a whole derives no benefit from tax provisions so loosely, even whimsically geared as inducements to new investment. Once more the only beneficiaries are the already very rich, who so far have shown no sign of becoming any more productive — only richer.

The next major Conservative tax initiative will take the form of the Poll Tax, to be levied on everyone over 18. A family of four adults on a minimum income will pay four times as much as the most wealthy aristocrats and businessmen in the country. It is the ultimate in regressive taxation, a measure that will increase inequality, and is meant to.

The new, harsh ideology of modern Toryism wants and needs inequality and justifies it as the essential prerequisite of economic success. In the brave new economic order there has to be unfairness if there is to be effectiveness. For them, the values upon which economic growth depends require rewards for risks and the real threat of deprivation as a minimal incentive at the bottom. Unequal rewards and benefits will make the most of the unequal abilities that people possess, and such measures as wage protection have no place, neither an economic rationale nor a social justification.

Fair taxation, in the new Tory view, has no place either. Any attempt at tax-mediated redistribution they tell us undermines incentive, and thrift, and savings and investment, and the more efficient use of labour and the optimal deployment of capital. The Thatcher argument is that those who seek to diminish inequality do so to the detriment of the common good, by depleting capital and discouraging enterprise. The victims in all this — so they say — are, in Tawney's words, not those upon whom taxation is levied but those for whom taxes are imposed.

Unexplained by the theory is the paradox of motivation. How is it that incentives for rich and poor are so very different? How can it be that for the rich the only stimulus to economic endeavour is that the rewards become increasingly lavish, while the poor are in continual need of the spur of their poverty?

'Does the Budget mark the end of the use of taxation to redistribute wealth?' Nigel Lawson was asked in 1988. 'I hope so. I hope we are in for a new era for this country,' he replied. The implication is a commitment to regressive taxation, an omen that every tax should resemble the Poll Tax, visited equally upon rich and poor. As inequalities in Britain widen, it is worth examining the evidence concerning inequality as an instrument of economic policy. Does the deliberate increase of inequality advance any recognisable economic goal?

It has been claimed that top rate tax cuts would increase savings and stimulate investment. Taxes were cut but investment did not respond as advertised. Britain was investing more in itself when taxes were higher. It was claimed also that top rate tax cuts would provide a long-needed boost to the economy. A recent City study showed that the UK tax windfalls of 1988 would be most appreciated by expensive hotels in far-off places, and by the foreign manufacturers of imported luxury goods.

Top rate tax cuts would also, it was hoped, reverse the brain drain. High tax rates had driven talent abroad and low rates would lure it back, in theory at least. This has not happened. The best and brightest of British science and technology, middle earners not greatly affected by Mr Lawson's rich man's bonanza, are leaving as never before, because chronic underfunding of the higher institutions in which they work has compelled them to work far below their potential. It is not poor personal remuneration but the slow strangulation of Britain's research effort that loses us our scientists.

And top rate tax cuts would also solve social problems by increasing giving to charity. That too has failed to happen. The poor, of whom there are many, give proportionately five times as much of their income to charity as do the rich, of whom there are few. And for reasons not unrelated to the increase of inequality, the growth of poverty over the last ten years has vastly outstripped the growth of charity.

Top rate tax cuts would increase efficiency, it was said. People would work harder if they were allowed to keep more of the rewards. But at the level at which the top rate tax cuts matter most, the most likely consequence of increased affluence is increased leisure. If an executive's golf handicap is a measure of a certain kind of efficiency, then minor increases in efficiency may have to be conceded to have resulted from tax cuts.

All the respectable evidence shows that higher levels of taxation are a much overrated disincentive. Japan has higher corporation and capital taxes than we have. Germany has higher taxes on investment income. Sweden and Austria have higher income taxes. And their economies, without the advantage of North Sea oil, have been more successful than ours. Indeed a quick look round the world's more advanced economies shows that throughout the post-war era it has been largely those countries with the most generous public spending and the best welfare provision, coupled with fair taxes, that have done best.

The final argument in favour of the new dispensation is that as the rich have become richer the poor have benefited too. In July 1988, Mrs Thatcher said that 'figures show that people at the lowest levels of income have gained on average more in standards of living than the overall average in the United Kingdom'.

Both Mrs Thatcher and Mr Lawson have justified the growing inequality in Britain by arguing that the poor are better off. The policy, Mrs Thatcher said in 1980, 'means more inequality but it means you drag up the poor people because there are more resources to do so'. 'It's not that we're deliberately saying the gap must widen,' the Chancellor said in 1988. 'I am concerned that the poor should be better off, and the poor being better off matters more than what the gap happens to be between rich and poor.'

The fact is that since 1979 the real living standards of the nation's 4 million poorest households have actually fallen, and by 6%. In the most up-to-date analysis based on official statistics, John Hills has discovered that once indirect taxes, price rises and benefit cuts are taken into account the losses to the poorest 4 million households average £2.30 a week. One reason is the unfair impact of indirect taxes which take up a

larger share of the income of the poorest 20%. These are the figures
from 1979 to 1986: since then social security changes have taken place.

Changes in Real Incomes 1979–86

	Bottom 4m	Next 4m	Next 4m	Next 4m	Top 4m
Cash:	−£2.30	+£1.30	No gain	+£1.70	+£64
%:	−6%	+2%	No gain	+8%	+26%

Estimated change in Real Incomes 1979–88

%:	−6%	+5%	+2%	+13%	+38%

If, as most agree, inequality continued to grow after 1986 at the same
rate as between 1979 and 1988 the position of the bottom 20%
remained as bad. No longer can Mrs Thatcher claim that all have
benefited from her period in power: the poor have become poorer as
inequalities have grown.

Greater inequality is the interests neither of the poor, nor of the
nation. For decades after 1945 there was a consensus that greater
equality enhanced opportunity and improved efficiency; that the
elimination of poverty augmented total purchasing power to the benefit
of industry; and that political liberty, economic opportunity and social
security were mutually reinforcing. A decade of Thatcher in power has
destroyed that consensus. For her and her government it is not full
employment and a decent provision of social security that are the
guarantors of liberty in our society, but that liberty itself consists in the
promotion of *laissez faire* economics and a growing inequality in society.

The results of these policies are all around us, and there seems no end
to the further inequalities the Conservatives seek. Their social policy is
moving rapidly towards the grudging dispensation of a politically
acceptable minimum of social welfare, as charity rather than as of right,
in place of what went before and strove, however imperfectly, to
integrate the poor in a productive and prosperous society. And for the
rich, there is the rationalisation and sanctification of greed: the few, in
the absence of any moral justification or empirical economic evidence,
will continue to increase their advantages over the many.

Left-Out Britain

Britain's Poor

'. . . a little more compassion is needed.'

Viscount Whitelaw

However hard it is to imagine Mrs Thatcher standing on the steps of Downing Street ten years ago proclaiming 'Where there is wealth, let us create excess. Where there is need, let us create hardship. And where there is poverty, let us create downright bloody misery,' that is exactly what she has done.

The Thirties are remembered for the thousands of the despairing unemployed who stood around on street corners day after day. The Eighties will be remembered for their own lost generation, the teenagers born in the late Sixties and early Seventies for whom there is neither unemployment benefit nor employment. In Britain now, thousands of them sleep rough in 'cardboard cities'. The Eighties will be remembered too for the creation of a state charity, the Social Fund; for the return of the pauper's funeral; for the impoverishment of hundreds of thousands of the elderly and for the imposition of an arbitrary and regressive Poll Tax.

In the Eighties new titles, labels and personnel have had to be invented to administer the harsh day-to-day realities of Mrs Thatcher's Britain: the Poll Tax Registration Officer, the Social Fund Officer, the Specialist Claims Control Team and the 'super snooper'.

Despite all talk of an economic miracle, there is now, as we approach the end of the Eighties, more poverty, worse poverty and more deepening poverty in the United Kingdom. There have always been poor elderly people because 'the poor get old and the old get poor', but it is to our shame that pensions now represent a smaller fraction of average earnings than they did in the Forties. Benefits for the unemployed have fallen too, being a smaller fraction of the average wage now than they were in the Thirties. Wage protection legislation that had survived from Victorian times has been swept away and financial support for children is now lower than at any time since the Fifties. And direct state support as of right has given way to the uncertain availability of discretionary help from the Social Fund, with a loan more likely than a grant. Needy citizens must now beg and borrow from the state.

For the first time since 1945 charity appears in our social security legislation, with the new Social Fund Officers being obliged to check that claimants have first exhausted the possibility of aid from local benevolent organisations and welfare funds. Even before the Social Fund was created, rulings had been made that characterised the new official Britain of the late Eighties. A mother, refused help for her son, was told that he did not need shoes to attend school. A pensioner, denied assistance to buy a replacement cooker, was told she did not need heated food.

As David Donnison has written of the Thatcher years, 'the boundaries which divide the politically thinkable from the unthinkable have been significantly altered'. More people are in difficulty, and in seeking help they encounter difficulties that were unimaginable ten years ago. And when official help is not forthcoming, unofficial sources flourish. The growth of illegal money-lending is an ugly, obvious consequence of the state's new miserliness.

There is widespread absolute poverty. Last year an estimated 125,000 were homeless, more without a roof over their heads than even a hundred years ago. In 1987, the most recent year for which full figures are available, 89,000 households had their electricity disconnected and 160,000 had automatic deductions from their basic benefit to pay electricity bills. In the same year 60,778 had their gas disconnected and 138,000 had to pay gas bills via automatic benefit deduction because they were in debt. In 1985 nearly two million county court actions were raised by creditors against people who owed money. In 1987 a third of council tenants were behind with rent payments. 2.4 million people were estimated to be living below the level set for income support or supplementary benefit.

These are the figures for those facing destitution. The figures for those in poverty, even by the government's own stringent criteria, are much higher. There are now four million individuals on income support, seven million who depend on it, nine million on low wages and

16 million or more living at income levels even government ministers have to describe as low.

Table 1   Growth in the number of people and children living in or on the margins of poverty in Great Britain between 1979 and 1985

	Persons			Children		
	1979	1985	% increase since 1979	1979	1985	% increase since 1979
Below SB	2,090,000	2,420,000	16	290,000	360,000	24
On or below SB	6,070,000	9,380,000	55	1,180,000	2,250,000	91
140% SB level or below	11,570,000	15,420,000	33	2,370,000	3,540,000	50

Comparisons with Europe are hard to come by, but an official estimate has now been made by the European Commission. Its figures, based on evidence from the British government, show that in the ten years from 1975 there was a doubling of poverty in the UK, from just over 3 million to 6.5 million. By European standards our nation is becoming steadily poorer. In 1975 Britain suffered less poverty than Luxembourg, Belgium, Italy and Germany. Now it has more than each of them. 12% of the UK population is now officially recognised as living in poverty. In Belgium the figure is 7.2%, in Germany 8.5%, in Luxembourg 7.9%, in the Netherlands 7.4% and in Italy 11.7%. Britain has moved from having 10% of Europe's poor in 1975 to having 15% today.

Poverty does not concern Mrs Thatcher. 'Abundance rather than poverty has the legitimacy which derives from the very nature of creation,' she told the Church of Scotland in 1987, dismissing as irrelevant centuries of Christian concern about the poor. She went on to cite, misleadingly out of context, St Paul's advice to the Thessalonians, that 'If a man shall not work he shall not eat.' 'Remember the woman with the alabaster jar of ointment,' she advised the puzzled Assembly, most of whom would be aware she was drawing attention to Jesus's subsequent reminder about the poor, with us always.

Under Mrs Thatcher not only have the numbers of the poor risen dramatically but government legislation has ensured that the poor will never have a share in any increased prosperity that may come the way of the nation at large. This is the main effect of the dissociation of the levels of pensions and insured benefits from those of average earnings. The government is now saving 4 billion pounds a year, a total of 18 billion pounds since 1979. A great many people are a lot poorer as a result.

Pensions, now linked to prices rather than earnings, have fallen back steadily and are now £12 a week behind the target set in the Seventies. Unemployment benefits have now been taxed and reduced, and undergone further attrition for many by means of the removal of the earnings-related component. An unemployed person may now receive only half of what he or she might have received in 1979. Income support levels have been redefined and then reduced by the obligation to pay 20% of rates or the Poll Tax, or to pay off loans borrowed for household necessities from the new Social Fund. Teenagers at 16 and 17 have been denied benefits altogether in a harsh US-style solution to the problems of teenage poverty.

Little of this was foreshadowed in 1979. In that year Patrick Jenkin, then Social Security Minister, said that pensioners would share in the rising standards of living of the country. There was no suggestion then that the earnings-related unemployment benefit would be removed, or that the real value of many benefits would decline; that benefits would cease to be linked to average earnings or that hundreds of thousands of teenagers would find themselves excluded.

Neither in 1979 nor in 1983 was there any suggestion that the death grant or the maternity grant would be abolished, or that SERPS, the state earnings-related pension scheme, would be downgraded. Indeed in October 1983, only months before he attempted to abolish it, Mr Norman Fowler said he had 'no plans' to take SERPS away. Yet in 1985 a greatly weakened version of SERPS was retained only after public pressure became intense.

In 1979, 1983 and again in 1987 no senior Tory was publicly suggesting that child benefit would be frozen or reduced in value. The manifesto promised that child benefit 'would continue to be paid, as now'. But despite that promise the Chancellor decreed in 1987 that the benefit would be frozen, admitting later that its existence would be guaranteed only until the next election and against his own advice, simply because there had been a minor punctuation error in that sentence in the manifesto concerning child benefit. Many families will be grateful that, in a struggle between the Chancellor and a comma, the comma won.

As a direct result of the policies of this government, poverty has increased. And it has increased even despite government attempts to improve the statistics on poverty by altering its definition. Under this government the national minimum has been lowered to a level at which it is insufficient to make ends meet. Of course the Tories have always denied this. They say instead that there can be no exact definition of what constitutes a poverty line and that therefore no one can identify a true and useful national minimum. There is now no satisfactory definition, Mrs Thatcher tells questioners who want to get at the facts about poverty.

If you want to deny a problem exists you can always assert that it defies definition, but almost ten years ago a Tory Minister, Lynda Chalker, then at Social Security, was more forthcoming: 'It is not sufficient to assess poverty by absolute standards. Nowadays it must be judged on relative criteria, by comparison with other groups in the community . . . Beneficiaries must have an income that enables them to participate in the life of the community.'

This was a clear rejection of 'starvation' or 'destitution' standards of defining who is poor. Mrs Chalker was simply admitting that the poor were not just those who faced starvation or were deprived of the most basic necessities of life: food, clothing and accommodation. It was not enough to avoid starvation; people must be properly fed. It was not enough to avoid homelessness; homes must be sound and free of damp and not sub-standard. It was not enough just to avoid hypothermia; adequate heating was necessary.

If we adopted one definition of those at or near the margins of poverty — an income level at 140% of the income support level — more than 15 million British citizens would be defined as being in poverty today. This represents an increase of 4 million since 1979. The 1979 definition is not lax. If its standards were applied today single claimants would have only £48.90 weekly after paying rent, married couples only £76.70. It would be an income level at much less than half the published figure for the average household income in Britain.

But would that allow families and individuals the opportunity, in the words of the 1979 minister, to 'participate fully in the life of the community'? As Peter Townsend has put it, poverty is more than simply a very low week-to-week money income. It is also 'the lack of resources necessary to permit participation in the activities, customs and diets commonly approved by the community'.

In Townsend's view, 'Individuals, families and groups in the population can be said to be in poverty when they lack the resources to obtain the types of diet, participate in the activities and have the living conditions and amenities which are customary or at least widely encouraged or approved in the societies to which they belong.'

The largest group of today's poor is the unemployed and their families. The second largest is formed by pensioners, so that the profile of poverty today, in 1989, is very similar to that of the Thirties. Pensioners have had a raw deal. There was no mention in 1979 of the possibility that ministers would break the link between pensions and average earnings, but that is exactly what they did. At the time of the decision to do so Sir Geoffrey Howe made another promise: 'Of course we want to be able to do more but we realise that that depends on the strength of the economy . . . I am confident that as our economy improves it will be possible to do more and ensure that pensioners share in the increase in national prosperity.'

Ten years have passed during which persistent claims have been made about the achievement of an economic miracle. Yet pensions remain frozen alongside last year's price levels, thus ensuring that over these ten years single pensioners are now £11.40 worse off and married couples £18.10 worse off. Under the 1974–79 Labour government the real value of the pension rose 20%. Since 1979 the increase has been only 2.2%. In June 1974 the British pension represented 19.8% of average earnings. In November 1978 it had risen to 20.4%. In April 1988 it had fallen to 17.2% and now it is just over 16%.

When all income is taken into account — dividends, savings, as well as occupational and other pensions — two-thirds of pensioner households have incomes less than £120 a week. While the average German worker received between 40% and 45% of earnings on retirement, a Frenchman 50%, a Belgian worker 60% and an Italian 80%, the typical British worker received only 34%.

Many of the pensioners who have escaped the worst effects of the downward drift in the value of the basic pension have done so as a result of the state earnings-related pensions scheme (SERPS) which the Conservatives wished originally to abolish but succeeded only in watering down. Certainly many pensioners have done better since 1979, mainly as a result of the contribution of occupational pensions, especially SERPS, to their income. SERPS additions, averaging 95p in 1979, rose to £23.95 in 1988 and will reach £40.50 by 1992. Yet but for vigorous lobbying and opposition the Tories would have destroyed the SERPS scheme.

In a rational world pension arrangements would be characterised by a strong government role and generous basic provision. Tory policy is one of fragmentation via company schemes and personal equity-based arrangements, with a gradually dwindling state-provided minimum as a safety net for the thriftless. There are strong arguments against this, not least from the *Financial Times*: 'A common presumption today is that the private sector can do everything better than the public sector. Pensions are an obvious counter-example. Pensions should meet two basic criteria. They should guarantee living standards in old age and they should not impede job mobility . . . Company schemes are incompatible with job mobility . . . personal portable schemes are flawed: they cannot guarantee living standards in old age because nobody can know what his contributions will eventually buy — it will depend on the vagaries of the stockmarket. In organising pensions the state is merely acting as a large and efficient clearing house.'

Pensioners have done badly in the Eighties, but it is the under-25s who have been singled out for the harshest treatment. The generation that must face and overcome the challenges of the 1990s is the very one that finds least favour in the eyes of the government. In April 1988 income support for 18 to 24-year-olds was cut by £7 a week. The under-18s lost even more, £14 a week. In September further restrictions meant that almost all 16 and 17-year-olds lost their right to basic income support. At a stroke 90,000 teenagers lost the right to benefit even when they were unable to find a 'guaranteed YTS place'.

For those who cannot find a place on a scheme, for those forced out of their parental homes through overcrowding, poverty, family discord or marital breakup, the prospects are now very bleak indeed. The social security system seeks to keep them at home, but once they have left home it frequently abandons them. With delayed payments, orders to move on and now further cuts in benefits to cover housing costs, more and more of Britain's young are becoming homeless.

The figures for the young homeless provide the most dramatic evidence of poverty among our young people. Around 150,000 are now estimated to be without permanent accommodation. The situation is worst in London, with perhaps 30,000 seeking a permanent home. 12,500 are squatting and almost 1,000 are reported missing in the capital. The misery, the cold, hunger, uncertainty and downright hopelessness that lie behind these figures can scarcely be imagined, and youth homelessness in Britain is now growing at a faster rate than anywhere in Europe.

These are Thatcher's children, the young people born in the late Sixties and early Seventies, who left school in the Eighties and whose political awareness is entirely confined to the period she has been in government. And thousands and thousands of them will enter the Nineties without every having had regular employment.

Shelter's most recent report records the tedium, despair and sometimes danger to life that ten years of Tory triumphalism have left in their wake. In more than 100 diaries kept daily by Britain's young homeless the real impact of the benefit changes and of youth unemployment are revealed, as in the story of a 19-year-old forced to sleep rough in London for over a year: he had 'looked everywhere for a place to stay but found nothing. It's cold sleeping in parks. I have claimed benefit from the DSS but have not received any money for six weeks.'

A young woman, forced to leave her home in the Midlands after being sexually assaulted by her brother, wrote: 'I wonder if people like the Prime Minister have been hungry, without a roof over their head, or disowned by their parents like us homeless people have been. I doubt it.' Such diaries, flatly devoid of hope, record the thoughts of what the government's own Social Security Advisory Committee last year called 'a class of homeless and rootless young people who are unable to return to the parental home and who cannot remain long enough in one location to find permanent accommodation or a job'.

Their plight, even as discerned through civil service prose, is desperate. They are teenagers at risk on a scale never before encountered. Without income or on the meagrest levels of income support, many of them homeless, many in crowded, dirty and dangerous bed and breakfast accommodation, they glimpse Britain's uneven prosperity only through shop windows. However much they wish to participate, to earn their way, they cannot. They are a new, excluded sub-class.

Yet it is they to whom the country will look in the 1990s, when an inexorable demographic change dictates that the number of new workers leaving school and entering the labour market will fall drastically. Thatcher's children — excluded, understandably embittered and without any sense of ever having contributed to or participated in the society into which they were born — may be unable to respond when jobs become available and their wasted talents are needed. A generation may have been tragically wasted, and Britain will have cause to regret the way it has been treated.

The disabled too have been added in increasing numbers to the growing total of the poor. The most recent Office of Population Censuses and Surveys report found that of Britain's 6.2 million disabled adults, 4 million were living within or at the margins of poverty. The average net income of a disabled adult is £82.20 a week — only one-third of average earnings.

The welfare state as originally conceived and as broadly agreed for 30 years included not only a safety net but a right to educational opportunity, to health care and to decent housing. Today's Conservatives have rejected government responsibility for these rights, absolving themselves of moral and financial obligations accepted by every British government since the war, withdrawing public spending from basic services such as housing.

But the assumption behind Tory policy — that public expenditure is bad for individuals and bad for the economy — is unproven by any British or foreign experience. In other chapters health and education are considered in detail. In this one housing policy and its effects on the lives of millions will be examined.

In 1979 there were 1 million on housing waiting lists in England. Now there are 1.29 million. During 1989 100,000 more families will become officially homeless. While the Housing (Homeless Persons) Act has helped 2 million people since its implementation, and dramatically reduced the numbers of children who have had to be taken into care, it is not comprehensive in the protection it offers, failing young people and women especially, nor is its future secure.

Homelessness and waiting lists are rising because fewer new homes are being built in the public sector, with only 17,800 built for rent last year. Even after private sector completions are included, Britain has been building fewer houses than it was in 1979. Other comparable countries have simply built more, completing anything from 25% to

100% more over the same period. Government ministers like to blame
local authorities for this miserable record, citing various inefficiencies
but the independent Audit Commission has concluded that financial
support has been so poor that 'even with efficient management
authorities are unable to perform their statutory duties adequately'.

Little in the way of building has been undertaken and little progress
has been made in improving housing amenities. Although less than 3%
of Britain's homes lack basic amenities, twice that proportion are
classified as 'unfit', and many more are in a state of disrepair. (The
figure is known and the government refuses to publish it: an informed
estimate puts it at an additional 5.5%.)

The Association of District Councils put the bill for overdue repairs
at around £86 billion, yet government subsidies are now worth only
around £420 million. Money for New Town housing has been halved
and the value of help for housing associations has remained static. Such
money as is available is being channelled towards a perverse response
determined by ideological commitment to the private sector. More
energy is now being expended on attracting private landlords into the
area of renting accommodation than on stimulating the more enduring
and dependable public sector. One private sector enthusiast, Lord
Caithness, an Environment Minister, has even gone so far as to suggest
a return to 'company homes'.

The need for low cost housing in both public and private sector is
greater than ever, as thousands of young people find themselves unable
to buy or rent. A recent survey found that almost 50% of London and
South-East households could not afford to be first-time buyers. 70% of
18 to 29-year-olds do not earn enough to pay for the average first
mortgage. Yet with increases last year of £50 a month for the average
mortgage of a first-time buyer — and increases of £75 in the South-East
— owner occupation is now beyond the reach of more and more people.

Millions find housing hard to afford, and many changes in benefit
regulations have eroded the incomes of those already struggling. Seven
million mothers and several million children were affected by the
decision to freeze child benefit, and the long-term future of child benefit
is seen to be at risk as its value falls. In order to save £150 million
charges for eyesight tests and dental checks were introduced. And rates,
from which poorer claimants were once exempt, must now be paid, in
the form of the Poll Tax, by all, however poor. The Social Fund was set

up to cover the withdrawal from death and maternity grants and the million single payments and two million additional payments, mainly for heating and urgent need expenses, that once covered everything from help with hospital bus fares to the provision of basic items such as cookers to the households of the very needy.

In place of these came the biggest extension of means testing and unaccountable bureaucratic power since the establishment of the welfare state. The lifebelt of DHSS support was replaced by the dead weight of Social Fund loans. Confidential guidelines which preceded the Fund made the true intentions of the scheme quite clear. The basis of its operation would be 'discretionary and judgemental'. The elderly and the disabled might be eligible for state financial support to continue in their homes and avoid institutionalisation, but not where 'other means such as help from local authority, relatives or charities' could be obtained. Nothing was to be given to children in need until family charity and all other local sources had been exhausted. When help was sought with funeral costs the state 'will make clear the style of funeral that will be met'. Only a plain coffin would be paid for, and the undertaker's and the chaplain's costs, but not the cost of a private plot. And those who could not afford to repay Social Fund loans would simply not receive them.

Local Social Fund officers are told that 'even when unable to help with a loan this should not prevent them trying to offer advice on coping with any continuing budgeting problem'. A government that has created poverty on a scale unknown since the Thirties but which refuses to acknowledge its responsibilities might be expected to redefine it at the moment of refusal of help as a 'continuing budgeting problem'. The assumption is that it is not the benefit that is inadequate but the beneficiary; that the state is blaming the poor, when on all the international evidence their poverty is a matter not of their choice but the government's.

The unemployed must endure not only the poverty the state has inflicted upon them, but also its arrogance and intrusiveness in the way it polices the social security system. This, particularly for single parents, can involve indignities and humiliations that have become almost routine.

All the unemployed are liable to have their claims checked by a new elite of claims control officers. They may be summoned for review at the unemployment benefit office or be asked to undergo medical examination. They are advised to visit retraining centres and their benefit can be reduced if any job offered is refused. Claimants must prove in detail that they have been applying for jobs.

A total of 5,000 DHSS staff are attached to one fraud investigation or another, 30 times as many as are employed in the far more serious area of tax evasion. Another 1,500 are employed as unemployment review or liable relative officers. A further 1,500 are employed as local office fraud officers and another 500 as special investigators in regional teams. Within the Department of Employment are another 650 offices whose job it is to detect fraudulent claims, and 100 attached to regional benefit teams on special exercises.

These specialist claims control operators are the *corps d'élite* of snooperdom, instructed to 'maximise recorded savings'. Their 10,000 known calls a year on *innocent* British citizens constitute menace rather than assistance. Techniques such as shadowing and surveillance, checks with neighbours, the police and other government departments and even searches of personal belongings have led, as even the Department admits, to 'allegations of harassment and bullying'.

The unemployed who are fit, who have a skill, a record of self-employment or even relatives who are known to be in business or self-employment are targeted for special attention. Single parents are targeted where 'no information is held regarding the identity of the father and his whereabouts are not known' and against whom 'the claimant refuses to take proceedings for maintenance'. Other candidates for targeting are those who have children 'of an age which would enable the mother to take up work' — a sentiment that makes happy assumptions about the rewards of job-seeking in 1989.

Simply because they meet these criteria individual single mothers are the random targets for early morning visits to establish whether or not they have sexual relationships. Investigators are instructed to check 'What explanation has been given to account for the presence of male items? Has this occurred frequently?' With no formal statutory powers of search, investigators are officially instructed to insinuate their way into the homes and even bedrooms of ordinary and more than ordinarily vulnerable citizens to check on clothes, shoes and even underwear.

So underhand were some of the methods used that in 1983 the Social Security Minister had to remind his investigators that certain approaches, such as impersonating officials from other departments, referring to non-existent poison pen letters and telling lies to trap claimants, were not permissible. But since the aim of all these efforts was not to obtain convictions but to secure the discontinuation of claims, pressure would suffice in cases where evidence was shaky or inconclusive. Much embarrassment, misery and poverty could result from unwitnessed pressures applied to vulnerable people under acute stress. Unsupervised officials might function simply to frighten people off benefit without any proper scrutiny of the circumstances.

A world has been created in which to be healthy and unemployed is to come under suspicion, where simply to be a single parent with school-age children is to be selected for close personal investigation. It is a world where to be unable to explain articles of clothing in one's bedroom is to be found guilty without trial and condemned, a world where the real crime is poverty and the punishment is imposed without any formal examination of the evidence.

12

Women and Tory Family Policy

'The battle for women's rights has been largely won. The days when they were discussed and demanded in strident tones should be gone forever.'

Mrs Thatcher 1982

'We must strengthen the family.'

Mrs Thatcher 1980s

'A woman's work is never done.'

Mrs Thatcher 1988

Over the last ten years the effect of Tory policy has been not to alleviate the position of women but to make it worse. By removing protection for part-time workers — who are mostly women, by removing Wage Council protection for the low paid — again mostly women, by reducing support for careers and mothers with small children, and by breaking the pensions-earnings link, the Tories have made the lives of many thousands of women poorer and more difficult. And even women who have not found themselves at a financial disadvantage live in greater fear of violent crime and are more concerned than ever about the decline of state education and the threat to the National Health Service.

Women and their rights are at best a marginal concern of the Conservatives. In their eyes women at work are a useful reserve of labour, available and expendable, and women at home are also to be exploited — in the name of family policy.

Back in 1983 Mrs Thatcher sent her cabinet colleagues away for the summer recess with instructions to 'think about the family over the oliday'. The set of cabinet papers, never officially disclosed but now nown thanks to a leak, outline an idea of breathtaking cynicism and, the Tory mind, commendable symmetry: much of the welfare state ould be dismantled if the various responsibilities it has shouldered ould be handed back to the family. 'What can be done,' a document ked, 'to encourage families — in the widest sense — to reassume sponsibilities taken on by the state, for example the disabled, the derly and unemployed 16-year-olds?'

Also included were proposals to encourage mothers to stay at ome, a re-examination of the usefulness of the Equal Opportunities ommission and proposals for making parents responsible for some f the anti-social behaviour of their children. One parent families were be the subject of particularly close scrutiny, with a review policy to nsure that the state encouraged 'responsible behaviour by parents'.

Some of these ideas are now being openly discussed, others remain n the hidden agenda. Meanwhile, presentation has been subtle, tressing the positive. The family has been extolled, as has the woman's lace within it. In the words of the Prime Minister in 1988, 'the family the building block of society, it is a nursery, a school, a hospital, a eisure centre, a place of refuge and a place of rest ... And women un it.'

As the state withdraws the family — where it exists — will be ompelled to do more and more, and women at home will be saddled vith the burden of care that the state is preparing to shed; looking fter ageing parents no longer able to manage independently, relatives lischarged from hospital with mental illness or handicap, and teenagers vho, through no fault of their own, are unable to find work or afford o set up on their own.

Society's problems will be privatised, and families — in practice, vomen — made responsible. With astonishing effrontery, the law and rder party, after ten years in power, hugely increased policing budgets nd much pressure on sentencing policy, has decided that crime is family matter and that a new principle of parental responsibility pplies. Parents are to blame. In education too, the family finds itself eing asked to take responsibility for success where the state is failing. More time with the children, lots of nursery rhymes when they are ittle, goes Nanny Baker's prescription — while the schools crumble.

In Mrs Thatcher's view it is all equally simple. 'Compassion can't

be nationalised. It's individuals that count. A responsible society
one in which people do not leave it to the person next door to c
the job. It is one in which people help each other, where paren
put their children first, friends look out for neighbours, families f
their elderly members. That is the starting point for care and suppc
— the unsung efforts of millions of individuals, the selfless work
thousands upon thousands of volunteers.'

There is no doubt that families can and do care, and all tl
respectable survey evidence confirms that. But to congratulate famili
for their efforts, undertaken out of love and duty, selflessly and unsun
as she says, and then proceed to use that as a pretext for the withdraw
of the very support that enables them to carry on, and to fudge ov
the inadequacies of community health and social services, and as
means of rationalisation of the closure of mental hospital wards
old people's homes — all that is betrayal of the family rather tha
an enhancement of its role.

The family is neither a universal nor an inexhaustible provision an
any policy that pretends otherwise is cruel deception. In the words
Roy Parker, Professor of Social Administration at Bristol Universit
'The political rhetoric is an effective manoeuvre to deflect attentio
from other kinds of analysis. It is an effective way of converting publ
issues into private issues.'

Yet the family, of which so much is to be expected, is changin
rapidly in response to internal and external pressures. The Tori
seek no understanding of this, but stick to broad assertions such a
'We must strengthen the family', and fail to deliver practical hel
even where its value is undisputed. For example, marriage guidanc
in London is grinding to a halt because of lack of funding. Coupl
in distress and in search of urgent help are offered appointmen
months ahead, if at all. Marriages, families and children suffer as
result. As the National Children's Homes Director of Social Wor
has stated, 'There's no public funding for this kind of work. Th
government has reduced its grants to the small number of scheme
we're running. But it is perfectly clear that if there was an effectiv
counselling system available a proportion of the families breaking u
could be reconciled.'

But slogans are cheaper than effective help, families go under, an
it is in the treatment of women as single parents that the government'

prejudices have become most obvious. The numbers of single parents have doubled over the last ten years and will double again in the fairly near future. The numbers of children in single parent families have also doubled and children in one parent families are at a much higher risk of poverty than children with two parents. 12% of two parent families are at or below income support level, a figure bad enough in itself. The figure for single parent families is more than five times that, at 65%.

The government's response has been predictable. It is as though a decision has been taken to misunderstand the problem and to justify a crude, intrusive and inappropriate response to it. The official line is that the problems arise from semi-voluntary pregnancy among single teenagers, to which the authoritarian response is near-punitive: rigorous restriction of benefits, intrusive means-testing and the implication that somehow the family should manage whilst the errant teenager finds a job and goes out to work.

Evidence to the Social Security Reviews stressed this kind of thinking, which is in keeping with policies being canvassed in the USA by the right-wing Heritage Foundation. Teenage mothers who leave home should suffer loss of benefit because, as every saloon-bar sociologist knows, 'they only do it for the council house and all the benefits'. Yet this obsession with teenage mothers in council flats simply does not match the facts. Only one single parent in five has never been married. Most lone parents have lost their partners through separation, divorce or death. The figures are available, yet in January 1989 the government launched a study based on a sample of single parents gleaned from one benefit office in every ten to 'explore why people become lone parents'. The tut-tutting and finger-wagging goes on. In the words of Mr John Moore, the government needs to be 'wary of providing incentives to obtain a particular benefit which can erode the sense of personal responsibility and adversely distort behaviour'.

There is no doubt that the vast majority of the 65% of single parents who rely on drawing income support would rather not do so, but they are confronted with the dilemma of whether to stay at home and look after their children or to attempt to find work and affordable child care too. Their experience is a world away from that of the Prime Minister, whose views as a working mother perhaps reflect more her status as a rich man's wife. 'We support the right of women to choose their own lives for ourselves . . . many women wish to devote themselves mainly to running a family and running a home, and we should have that choice too.'

Or as she put it on another occasion, 'It is possible [for a woman] to run a home and continue with a career provided that two conditions are fulfilled. First, her husband must be in sympathy with her wish to do a job. Secondly, where there is a young family the joint income of husband and wife must be sufficient to employ a first-class housekeeper to look after things in the wife's absence. The second is the key to the whole plan.' So there we are.

Others see it differently, and Britain's child care for less well-heeled working mothers is among the worst in Europe. A recent study by the European Commission's Childcare Network found that 'on virtually every policy indicator this country comes near the bottom'. Bronwen Cohen and Peter Moss of the Childcare Network state that, 'The UK, together with Ireland and the Netherlands, has the lowest level of publicly funded child care in Europe . . . Just over 40% of three- and four-year-olds go to school, but half of this figure consists of four-year-olds admitted early to primary school, itself a questionable policy, while most of the remaining 23% are children attending nursery education part time, a provision of little use to working parents. Out of school care is non-existent in most areas. Uniquely in Europe, the UK does not offer maternity leave to all employed pregnant women as of right.'

There are two types of under-fives child care, nurseries and child-minding. 80% of UK parents at work use child-minders, according to the EEC publication *Caring for Children*, but only 3% believe this to be the best provision. Full-time local authority day nursery care, however, covers only just under 4% of three- and four-year-olds.

In France, Luxembourg and the Netherlands, tax allowances are offered to help cover child care costs. In contrast, care in Britain's workplace nurseries is taxed, and taxed more heavily than the ubiquitous company car. Mrs Thatcher has strong views on the subject and has recently stated that tax allowances for child care would lead to 'the most terrible abuses'. The Employment Minister, Patrick Nicholls, agrees, saying it is not the government's job to provide a creche system. And Mr John Patten, the man in charge of government policies for women, also concurs. 'My very strong feeling is that we do not want to see massive state or employer provided nurseries. What is needed is small-scale local provision ... There is a vast pool of untapped provision among men and women who are at home — or could be at home — and help sort out these sort of services.'

Until now mothers seeking reliable child care to cover their working hours could depend on child-minders being subject to inspection by the local social services and being registered with them as offering safe and adequate premises and supervision. Now the government intends, in the current Children's Bill, to deregulate child care for the over-fives, which will greatly add to the anxieties of the working mother. As Jo Richardson, Labour's shadow spokesperson on women's affairs, says, 'Encouraging women to leave their children in the care of others while removing regulation of child care premises for over-fives is downright dangerous'.

The inadequacy of child care in Britain is instrumental in maintaining the second-class status of women at work. Forced to work part-time, juggling work with child care, they face uncertainties, subordination and poor remuneration that only safe, high-quality, flexible and affordable child care will remedy. Market forces and amateur voluntarism have nothing to offer. Only a coherent and properly funded government policy to encourage local authorities and employers to meet this challenge will release the full potential of working mothers.

As things are, they move in and out of the labour market, their careers frustrated, their contribution limited not only by poor child care arrangements but by Britain's uniquely poor arrangements for parental leave when children are born. The UK is the only EEC country to have no legal provision for parental leave equally available to mothers and fathers. In addition, UK workers have no right to take time off to look after sick children. The UK is the only state to have allowed maternity provision to deteriorate in the Eighties, limiting reinstatement rights and eligibility while other countries have actually improved them.

In the UK 54% of pregnant women are eligible for maternity leave. West Germany gives all mothers 40 weeks maternity leave on 80% pay, Denmark 18 weeks on 90%, Holland 12 weeks on 100% and Greece 12 weeks on 50%. A European initiative to help working mothers and families generally, the Parental Leave directive, would provide three months full or six months part-time paid leave over and above maternity or paternity leave and would greatly improve the security and status of British working women. Unfortunately for them the British government, alone in Europe, opposed the draft directive

During the last ten years Child Benefit, the one benefit paid exclusively to women, has been frozen. Its future is now in doubt The maternity grant has been abolished, making Britain the only country in Europe with no item of universal maternity provision. In child care provision and in the field of maternity and paternity rights Britain is now just about at the bottom of the European league. Once again the party that supports the family has gone to extraordinary lengths to avoid doing so. Over the years the government has fought every attempt to extend the invalid care allowance to married women and capitulated only when faced with the prospect of certain defeat in the European courts.

Increasingly women have had to work but, despite the theoretical protection of the provision of equal rights legislation, their treatment in the workplace has in practice reinforced their second-class status there. Although 70% of working women throughout the EEC now work full-time, women in Britain form the vast majority of the part-time workforce. And the government has sought to reinforce the traditional image of women workers: peripheral, easily displaced into the domestic role and maintaining only a temporary and insecure hold on paid employment.

Still segregated into the lowest paid, lowest status, most insecure sectors of work, women are paid at rates on average less than three quarters of those for men. Three out of every four of the low paid are women. Three out of every four covered by minimum wage legislation are women. And two out of every three who have now been removed from Wage Council protection are women.

No new rights have been won for women during the Thatcher years Instead the government has failed even to recognise the importance of women in the workforce. In May 1988 the Home Secretary, perhaps in an unusual interpretation of the title of his office, seemed to be suggesting that more mothers ought to stay at home. In that same month the Prime Minister argued the importance of motherhood over all else. Yet by the end of the year the Employment Secretary was declaring the Eighties to be the decade of women and noting the importance of 'the married returners to the labour market'. He was speaking, however, not from any pro-women sentiment but in response to compelling demographic change: between 1988 and 1995 the numbers of young people in the labour force will decline by more than one million. The efforts of women in the workforce, not previously encouraged, will then be essential.

A proper strategy for women would involve allowing women to develop their full potential — through training, with the support of adequate child care and via work opportunities. The removal of discrimination and the promotion of equal opportunities should be at the centre of community and working life, not a peripheral issue as it has been for the last ten years. Yet despite campaigns by women and sustained pressure from the Equal Opportunities Commission the government does little and refuses even to listen.

During the Seventies and Eighties the numbers of women in work increased from 8.2 million to 9.7 million. By 1995 it is estimated that around 12.3 million women will be working. The most dramatic increase has been in part-time work, the figure for that having risen to 4.3 million. In practice this means that these women are doing the jobs that are of lowest status and are least protected. And women employees generally receive fewer bonuses and less in the way of shift payments as well as lower basic pay.

Over a quarter of women (27% in 1989) with children under 5 go out to work. Increasing numbers (recently 25%) of women now return to work within a year of having a child. The biggest increase in employment among women has taken place in the age group 25–44, with two-thirds now at work and three-quarters expected to be working by 1995. Among working women, part-time working is commonest, at around 68%, for single parents. 40% of working married women work part-time, and only 21% of single working women. But such are the limitations in Britain in terms of child care arrangements, job opportunities and equal rights that we have one of the lowest employment rates in the industrialised world for women with children under five.

Women lag well behind in terms of pay. A recent survey by *Business* magazine found that only 2% of women earned over £40,000 per annum, compared to 7% of men. At the other end of the scale, one in five women in full-time employment earns less than £90 a week, compared to one in 30 men. On average women in the UK are still being paid 34% less than men. They do better in France, only 19% behind, and better still in Italy (17% less) and in Denmark (14%). In the whole of Europe only the women of Spain and Portugal fare as badly in terms of relative earnings.

Employment inequality is greater in Britain because, as the EEC's Social Action Programme states, there is a 'lack of adequate facilities for working mothers'. According to a 1980 survey from the Policy Studies Institute 40% of mothers felt unable to return to work because of lack of child care facilities and another 30% could not find work with hours compatible with their child care responsibilities. Better child care provisions and more flexible working hours could bring more than three mothers in every four back into employment.

The Tory record on employment rights for women is a disgrace. Not only have they failed to make improvements, they have stalled or vetoed attempts from Europe to improve a position which is, by international standards, indefensible. Such changes as have been made, for example the removal of the restrictions on women working in coal mines, are those which fit in with the government's laissez-faire inclinations. Nothing has been done that could be viewed as reflecting a coherent philosophy of rights for women workers.

Our first woman Prime Minister simply does not believe there is a problem. She is on record as saying 'Many women have opportunities but do not use them . . . or are too easily contented with the job that they are doing and do not necessarily make the effort to climb the tree'. Millions of British women do make the effort, and find that the government has time and time again failed to support them, as in January 1989, when Britain joined a number of other member states in blocking proposed European legislation that would have protected the rights of part-time workers.

Where improvements have occurred it has been because the government has been unable to oppose changes pressed upon it from Europe. Two such changes are the 1984 Equal Pay Act and the 1986 amendment. These brought Britain into line with the 1975 directive that women workers should be paid the same as men for doing work of equal value. Two of the most telling subsequent decisions have ensured that fringe benefits paid to women workers could not be used to justify paying them less and that provisions of the legislation could not be side-stepped by the employment of a token man in grades usually dominated by women.

As more women enter the labour force the disadvantages they face will be seen as more and more unjust. By 1995 about 800,000 more women between the ages of 25 and 44 will be working. It would be indefensible if the continuation of current employment practices, enshrining permanent low status, low pay and low security, were to be allowed to blight the endeavours of the very people whose recruitment into employment is expected to meet the crisis created by the fall in numbers of younger workers. But it is very difficult to see how any improvements are likely to occur under a Tory administration.

Even for women in secure full-time employment there is discrimination in almost every workplace, if not at entry then as time passes and the question of promotion arises. The recruitment of women into the professions of law, medicine and accountancy has doubled within a generation, with men and women coming in now in roughly equal numbers. Yet in the higher ranks of the civil service there are ten males for every female. For every female partner in a firm of solicitors there are 14 males and there are 25 males for every female on the judicial bench. Senior medical appointments are almost as unequally distributed. There is a smaller proportion of women in parliament than in the legislatures of all but four of the states of the Council of Europe.

The Prime Minister herself apart, women do not figure largely in public and political life. Even the 12-member advisory group on women's issues included only two women, and since the departure of Edwina Currie only one. Other advisory groups average one female member for every six males and at Downing Street the Prime Minister, in her own words, is 'surrounded by men'.

In education the opportunities that were created in the Sixties and Seventies are under threat, with the right-wing Social Affairs Unit pressing for a return to the teaching of 'girls as girls and boys as boys'. And the current push for educational reform and a national curriculum has done little to address the needs of girls.

Sex discrimination still occurs in interviews, according to a recent report in the Journal of Personnel Management. Promotion is liable to be slow for women. One study of Esso found that women graduates who joined the company were two grades behind their male counterparts after only six years. In accountancy only 0.5% of partners in London firms are women. Within the civil service women progress far more slowly than men. For example, half the men who joined the civil service in 1972 and remained in it had reached the senior grade five by 1987, in contrast with only 14% of the women.

It is now 13 years since the Equal Opportunities Bill became law, but when the Equal Opportunities Commission pressed for changes in the Act to bring it up-to-date the government refused. The Commission got no support for its proposals to give statutory backing to equal pay for work of equal value; to compel public bodies to eliminate sex discrimination; to strengthen employment protection for pregnant women (which included the abolition of the two-year qualifying period for protection from unfair dismissal); to reduce legal constraints on the Commission's own inquiries into discrimination; to abolish employers' rights to make legal representations against the issue of a non-discrimination notice; and to include provisions for a re-examination of the functioning of industrial tribunals in relation to cases involving equal pay or sexual discrimination, so that at least one woman sat on the tribunal. These reforms are overdue if only because, in the words of the Commission, 'nowhere can one find a comprehensive statement of the law relating to sex discrimination'.

Women caring for dependent relatives have done badly too. 15% of women, around 3.5 million, are identified as carers, such responsibilities being commonest among the 45–64 age group. 29% of single women in these middle years are carers, but the typical carer is no longer the unmarried daughter. The vast majority are married and their duties can be onerous, with survey evidence indicating that half are spending more than ten hours a week on the task, a quarter around 20 hours and 14% a gruelling 50 hours. Estimates of the total value of this kind of care range from £15 billion to £24 billion, and although most of it is provided by married women they have only recently (and as a result of the threat of European pressure) gained access to invalid care allowances previously available only to single carers.

The elderly, most of whom are women, have suffered both from the insidious pressures on the various forms of family and statutory care available to them and from the current attack on pensions. By breaking the link between earnings and pensions and by awarding pensioners an increase less than the current rate of inflation last

April, the Tories have inflicted a real cut in living standards upon the elderly, both men and women.

Women at risk of violence have had little help from the policies of the last ten years, and in many ways they are worse off. Conservative housing policies, obsessed with the owner-occupier, have greatly diminished the alternatives for the victims of domestic violence. Council waiting lists, longer than ever because of building cutbacks, offer no hope of permanent refuge and even hostel places — because of changes in benefit regulations — have become less available. There is in effect a housing trap that condemns many women to unending assault in the home.

Over the last ten years the incidence of violent crime has doubled. Rape has more than doubled. In some surveys nine out of ten women have said they are afraid to go out alone. Fear is widespread, both in the home ('I go home at four o'clock, lock myself in, never open the door after dark ... I've got three locks on my door but I still don't feel safe'), outdoors and on public transport.

A British Transport Police report on assaults on women travelling by rail was suppressed by British Rail. Perhaps the recent 25% cut in the number of guards would be less defensible if the facts were available. Official advice — the standard Tory alternative to effective action — to women travelling alone rings hollow: sit near other passengers; in buses sit near the driver or conductor; avoid using isolated bus stops. The advice ignores the realities: that women are more dependent on public transport than men; that bus conductors are a threatened species; that people cannot move house simply in order to make use of less isolated bus stops.

In general, the Tory push on crime has drifted further and further from crime and its underlying realities. The celebrated 'short sharp shock', with its emphasis on physical training, failed to reduce crime rates among the young (although it equipped a good number of them to run faster than policemen). When riots broke out in 1981 there was no official interest in the roots of mass disorder, no admission that recession, unemployment and hopelessness might have contributed, but instead an immediate focus on indiscipline in the home and the school, for which parents and teachers might be blamed. And with most crime committed by teenagers, no one in government has paused to reflect on the direct and indirect consequences of removing the benefit rights of 16 to 18-year-olds.

And now the family is being asked to bear individual responsibility for another vast collective failure. Parents will appear in court because, in the simplistic worldview of the 1987 Tory manifesto, 'the origins of crime lie deep in society; in families where parents do not support or control their children'. Never mind about the loss of benefit for teenagers and the individual and family poverty that has created. Never mind about the frustrations and disappointments, the aimlessness of life without a job and without any means of support. The poverty-induced drift to street life and petty crime is a family matter, because the family must be found guilty if the government is to be cleared.

Britain's first woman Prime Minister has done conspicuously little for Britain's women. Over the past ten years they have been treated mainly as a second-class labour reserve — available, cheap and disposable — in the workplace, and no better in relation to maternity and family rights and in the care of dependent relatives. As women re-enter the workforce in growing numbers the Conservatives ask not how employment can be made fair and attractive for them, but how that second-class labour reserve can be most cheaply adapted to fill the expected vacancies. Were it not for the continuous upward-tugging of European comparisons and the pressure of European legislation, Britain's women would be doing even worse. And is it not significant that among the few spontaneous Tory initiatives for women in the last ten years was one that allowed them back down coal mines after more than 100 years?

13

Unsafe in their Hands: The NHS

'. . . those who can afford to pay for themselves should not take beds from others.'

Mrs Thatcher, 31 January 1989

In 1982 Treasury civil servants were asked to prepare a statement of public spending needs for the coming ten years. Behind closed doors they gathered evidence and reported. There was no doubt that Britain needed to spend more on its Health Service. Nothing less than a real rise of 1.7% a year in hospital resources would be 'sufficient to provide for demographic change and inescapable medical developments, with a margin for small improvements in mental handicap services'.

But even that 1.7% would do little to cater for 'the pressing need for more resources'. Substantial cash injections were required 'to improve standards in the worst mental handicap hospitals, to make hip operations, transplants, dialysis, etc. more widely available and to introduce minimum standards in maternity care'. The officials concluded that 'expenditure would need to rise at 2–3% a year to make significant progress in all these areas'.

These were the resources the government's own advisers thought necessary. The Health Service is still waiting for them, and its needs continue to grow. The very young and the very old, age groups making relatively heavy use of the Health Service resources, have grown in number by around 19% and 20% respectively over the 1980s and official statistics suggest that births, and hence numbers of the very young, could rise even faster over the next decade. The additional resources required for demographic change alone, the civil servants concluded, had to be revised upwards to between 1.0% and 1.1%.

It is perhaps a sign of great concern within the civil service that the evidence and recommendations produced should be so damaging to the case being put by ministers, but that is what the civil servants found. Not only did they conclude that the current 1% allocated to cover all demographic and technical developments would 'barely maintain standards', they doubted whether much could be expected of 'efficiency savings', already criticised by the All Party Social Services Committee as 'backdoor cuts'.

Such savings could not be sustained throughout the Eighties, nor would Health Service charges solve the problem of the funding shortfall. 'Public expenditure cannot be substantially reduced by increasing income from charges within the present system of funding.' Without any new money the only possible means of reducing public spending on the Health Service would be, they concluded, 'radical changes within a tax-based system, e.g. new charges, withdrawing certain services or shifting part of the population, voluntarily or compulsorily, on to private health insurance'. Naturally, it was the intention of the government that these findings remain secret.

Since 1979 Conservative ministers have never given the NHS what it needs. Their real agenda is the obvious corollary of the stealthy public sector neglect they practise — the growth of private health care. Mrs Edwina Currie, when a junior Health Minister, made it clear when she said she wanted 'a thumping big growth in the private sector', in effect a trebling of the resources devoted to private medicine. 'If people have got the money,' she said, 'then I would encourage them to seek their health care elsewhere.' And in an illuminating exchange in the House of Commons, Mrs Thatcher has suggested that private health care, rather than the National Health Service, should become the norm for those who can afford it: 'Those who can afford to pay for themselves should not take beds from others.' The advance of private medicine, to be pursued by means of the destabilisation of the National Health Service, is the underlying theme of the government's latest health initiative, the White Paper on the NHS of January 1989.

Although government sources will admit privately that for the NHS even to stand still a 2–3% growth in funding every year is required, this has never been achieved under Mrs Thatcher. According to figures recently produced by Professor John Wells of Cambridge University, the mean growth rate for real NHS spending since 1979 is only 1.6%. This compares with the 3.6% achieved under the last Labour government and rates of between 2% and 4.6% under a variety of Labour and Conservative governments since the 1950s.

Under Mrs Thatcher a long period of improvement in Health Service funding has been brought to a halt. For 15 years from the mid-1960s real Health Service expenditure as a proportion of real national disposable income underwent a more or less continuous rise. Since 1981 this ratio has actually declined to a noticeable degree and capital investment — at around 5%, only a very modest fraction of total annual expenditure — has lagged just as much as recurrent spending on salaries, goods and services.

Given the growing demands made upon it and the lack of commensurate growth in funding, the NHS has since 1979 had to struggle harder and harder to provide a service to patients. And Britain does badly in comparison with other countries. Most have increased their health care spending as a share of national income over the Eighties, France by 1%, USA by 1.5%. Britain's health care funding has stagnated, and stagnated at an internationally low level. Health care receives a smaller share of national income in Britain than it does in almost all our major international competitors. Britain spends only 6%, compared with 7% in Canada, 8% in France and Germany and more than 10% in the USA. Only a huge boost for the NHS budget would bring us up from our present 6% to the OECD average of 7%. Currently our spending is on a par with that of Spain and Portugal and government ministers still insist it is too much.

Expenditure on health care as a percentage of GDP 1985

Country	Public	Private	Total
Belgium	5.5	1.7	7.2
France	6.7	1.7	8.4
Denmark	5.2	1.0	6.2
Germany	6.4	1.8	8.2
Greece	4.1	0.1	4.2
Ireland	6.9	1.6	8.0
Italy	5.4	1.3	6.7
Netherlands	6.5	1.8	8.3
Portugal	4.1	1.6	5.7
Spain	4.3	1.7	6.0
United Kingdom	5.2	0.8	6.0

WHERE THERE IS GREED . . .

Over the Eighties a larger proportion of what has to be spent on the Health Service has come from sources within the Health Service itself. Since 1978–79 money raised from sale of NHS land has risen from £7.5 million to £246 million. By 1988 more than £600 million had been raised from land asset sales. Not even the nurses' pension scheme has been immune from Treasury raiders. And efficiency savings, widely seen within the NHS as simply going without and regarded by the government's own civil servants as 'dubious', have become central to the financing of health care, as have commercial ventures within hospitals, such as shopping arcades and fast food concessions.

Something had to give. In late 1987 and early 1988 inadequate funding led to reductions in intensive care facilities for babies in St Mary's Hospital, Manchester, the closure of a children's cancer ward in St Bartholomew's, London, and waiting lists for urgent cardiac surgery in Birmingham. With all that and a group of surgeons actually advertising in a local newspaper to inform patients that because of cutbacks only emergencies could be admitted, the government had to respond. With an official fanfare celebrating unprecedented generosity, additional but still inadequate funding was released. Funding remains inadequate, as allocations for the coming year show. Once higher inflation, charges, and past salary commitments are taken into account, the government contribution has risen by only 1.5%, too little to keep pace with demography, technology and pressing needs.

286 hospitals have closed since 1979 and the pace of closures has increased over the last five years. Numbers of hospital beds have fallen from 361,670 in 1979 to only 315,000 today. We now have fewer beds than at any time since the 1940s and again international comparisons do not flatter us. We have around seven beds per 1,000 population, far fewer than most countries. France has 11.6, Germany 11.1, Sweden 14.0 and even Ireland 9.7.

Government apologists defend bed closures in terms of the inappropriateness of institutional care for many mentally handicapped and mentally ill patients. That would be acceptable only if community care for discharged patients was indeed adequate, but it is not. Many former psychiatric patients are left to fend for themselves, unsupervised and at risk, with only bed and breakfast provided.

Perhaps not surprisingly, waiting lists for surgery have risen again. There are now 731,826 people on hospital waiting lists in England, compared with 695,000 in 1979. Although the relationship between bed availability and waiting lists is a complex one, with staff and operating theatre availability also playing a part, bed shortages still abound in all significant areas.

And as funding inadequacies have begun to show up in the form of increasing shortages in established services they have also blighted all efforts to improve services in the areas targeted as priorities in widely approved policy documents such as *SHARE* and *SHAPE*. These identified services for the mentally ill and the mentally handicapped, services for the elderly and community-based services for favourable treatment in terms of resource allocation and planned extension. Little progress has been made because money has not been available.

One area in which the covert strategic drive towards privatisation has made progress is in the care of the elderly. The nursing home industry has boomed since 1979, providing for-profit care largely at public expense as a result of the increasing availability of DHSS supplementation for care in the private sector. The bill for the taxpayer has risen one hundredfold since 1979. Quality of care is difficult to ensure, with the profit motive driving standards down along with costs, and supplementation available only for nursing home care, not for increasing services to the frail elderly in their own homes.

The future development of services for the elderly — an important and vulnerable group of Health Service users whose numbers will rise significantly over the next 20 years — receives only minimal attention in the White Paper on the Health Service. Those who spent their working lives paying for a comprehensive Health Service and are now approaching a time of life when its provisions are of great importance to them, are at the same time showered with gratuitous advice about woolly hats and warned implicitly that they may be forced into private provisions for which they had not planned.

By a number of important and internationally accepted measures Britain's health statistics give rise to concern. In August 1986 the *British Medical Journal* commented on unpublished government statistics on variations in death rates between social classes over the Seventies and early Eighties. 'The differentials between classes I and II and classes IV and V and those between non-manual and manual social classes have widened. The mortality of men higher up the social scale has improved and that of those lower down the scale has deteriorated.'

A previously highly respected study of the effects on health of social deprivation, the Black Report, was not exactly suppressed, but was published in 1980 with minimal circulation in the course of a holiday weekend, carrying an uninvited official introduction stating that the cost of meeting its proposals was 'quite unrealistic in present or any foreseeable economic circumstances, quite apart from any judgement that may be formed of the effectiveness of such expenditure in dealing with the problems identified'.

While the Black Report recognised that the state of medical knowledge was such that it was not possible to spell out precisely all the causes of ill health in the context of deprivation, it drew clear conclusions about the direction of the available evidence. Deprivation helped explain the unfavourable health records of the poorest sections of British society and a serious attack on the problem would involve altering not just health but social security policy.

With the publication of *The Health Divide* in 1987, the government used its own figures to update the position and showed that the health gap between rich and poor was continuing to widen. For the lower socio-economic groups death rates for both men and women in middle life remained what they had been 30 or 40 years ago, and in the case of certain diseases actually increasing, while middle-class rates had improved substantially. Once again an adverse report on the nation's health caused controversy, and the Chairman of the Health Education Council attempted to stop a press launch.

The King's Fund Institute has highlighted research suggesting that 60–80% of the variations in death rates between different areas can be traced to socio-economic factors. The Institute also draws attention to the inadequate funding of health education and information. While some £180 million a year is spent on promoting drink, the government can find less than 0.5% of that to finance information on the risks of alcohol. The entire budget for health information and education amounts to only a miserly £38 million.

Official embarrassment is understandable. Other countries have done better by their health, France and Ireland, for example, showing striking improvements. In Britain, however, poor housing, poor working conditions and widespread poverty arising from high unemployment and poor social security provisions are reflected in internationally discreditable health statistics.

None of these major issues have been tackled. The preventive role of the NHS has been underfunded to the point of neglect, with the provision of well-women clinics still falling far short of public and professional expectations. Insufficient resources have been allocated to meet changing patterns of demand. The numbers of people over 85, who inevitably make heavy use of health and social services, will rise by 50% over the next 15 years but no special provision has been made for them. Among younger people the number of AIDS patients is doubling every ten months and although some additional funding has been made available it is not enough.

Despite the paucity of imaginative development and gradual erosion of important services over the last ten years in the NHS it remains a very popular national institution. Public support for it has been demonstrated in repeated surveys, including some that have shown that most people would forego tax cuts in order to ensure adequate funding for health care organised on a nationwide basis.

Before the Thatcher era few British citizens felt the need for private health care. In 1979 there were only 1.3 million subscribers to private medical insurance. Now there are 2.5 million subscribers and around 5 million people, about 10% of the population, covered. Only 8% of those who subscribe do so as individuals; 55% are covered by company schemes, 18% as employee schemes. Private health care is concentrated in the South, with coverage at 8% in London and 10% in the South-East, with only 3% coverage in Scotland and the North.

Most of those insured are healthy, since private care is not comprehensive and discriminates strongly by price against those with chronic or disabling conditions. Mrs Thatcher has admitted that if she were to be faced with serious illness she would avail herself of the services of the NHS. She would be wise to do so: private hospital care is neither extensive — less than 9,000 beds in hospitals sophisticated enough to carry out surgery — nor widely equipped for the care of the seriously ill.

Yet pressure on an area of Health Service activity most susceptible to the results of underfunding, namely elective surgery – operations such as hip replacement, hernia and varicose vein operations that are not urgent and can be delayed — has driven people into the private sector via long NHS waiting lists. 13% of elective surgery is now carried out in the private sector. In terms of the total activity of the NHS elective surgery represents only about 3%, but since waiting lists for it are a major political issue and the private sector can handle the 'planned turnover' involved it has proved an important opportunity for private sector growth.

There is no doubt about the general trend of Tory health policy. Fees have already been brought in for eyesight tests and dental checks, and hospital 'hotel bills' have been ruled out only until after the next general election. Other charges will be made by hospitals under White Paper proposals. Pay bed proposals, which allow private sector interests to make for-profit use of major NHS facilities and services, are likely to be expanded in a move quite separate from proposals for opting out by hospitals.

Many on the Right propose going much further. The Adam Smith Institute has already pressed for a £50 inducement for anyone taking out private health insurance and for charges for accommodation within NHS hospitals. The Institute, according to its document, *Omega Health Policy*, also wants charges for visits by family doctors, and for all drugs, family planning services and ambulance transport other than for emergencies.

Private medicine has already penetrated the Health Service quite substantially, and other private sector activity within it has increased with the contracting out of cleaning, catering and laundry services. Lotteries, raising sums that though large are quite insignificant in relation to the real cost of the NHS, have been welcomed by the Prime Minister. Private management consultants now take fees of £14 million a year, compared with only £400,000 in 1979.

Yet all the evidence, national and international, suggests that the best way of providing health care for anyone is to provide it for everyone. The National Health Service has proved itself not just to be fairer but more efficient, most cost effective and more economical in its use of resources as well. Despite propaganda about bloated bureaucracy, the NHS is administered with great economy. In Britain less than 5p in the £1 goes on administration. In America administrative costs in a purely private system are four times that, at 20%. France, with a hybrid public/private system, is still a lot higher than ours at 12%. Private care in Britain is more costly in administrative terms than the NHS, with BUPA spending 10p in the £1 and the Private Patient Plan 12p.

The latest US academic research concludes that it is 'undeniable that administrative costs in the US are considerably higher than those in Canada or Great Britain and that the potential savings from a national health programme are substantial'. One reason is that in America the number of administrators has risen three times faster than the number of medical staff. In Britain over the same period medical staff have increased in numbers at twice the rate of administrators.

And by the most basic of measures, the cost of care, the National Health Service has proved itself to be giving value for money. The best available research information suggests that hernia operations cost on average £600 in the NHS but around £1,200 in the private sector, that coronary bypass surgery costs £3,000 in the NHS but £7,500 in the private sector, that tonsil surgery costs around £600 in the NHS and around £1,000 in the private sector. Private hysterectomies and hip replacements cost respectively £600 and £700 more than NHS procedures.

But Mrs Thatcher is prepared to ignore the obvious and disregard the huge savings offered by public provision in order to grasp an opportunity to create new privilege. For the elderly particularly, private health care offers a very bad bargain. Companies are reluctant to take on customers liable to complex and costly illnesses, and this is reflected in the fees being discussed, perhaps as much as £1,000 a year to insure an older person for reasonable medical care.

The costs of private care are not simply the fees paid by companies and individuals. We all pay for it as the NHS loses 1,000 nurses a year to private hospitals. And we will pay more and more as Mrs Thatcher refuses adequate funding for the NHS and offers endless subsidies to the private sector in the form of tax relief for private medicine. As a result anything between £40 million and £200 million of public money will go towards the financing of private care.

In the face of all the evidence that the public sector can offer a comprehensive service and do the job better at less cost, government proposals are designed to bring private medicine to the heart of the NHS. The proposals for opting-out by hospitals will distance the local patient from his hospital, reducing his treatment to an item of trade with a distant facility. Self-governing hospitals, in order to survive, will have to adopt the mores of the private sector, discriminating against those whose treatment is liable to be unacceptably costly.

There are real fears, reported by the National Association of Health

Authorities, that hospitals will 'drop uneconomical services and inevitably concentrate on productive profitable services at the expense of services, say, for the elderly and the chronic sick'. Their submission states that treatment '. . . could have higher costs to patients and families in terms of travelling distances . . . Will hospitals concentrate on profitable services which are in demand by purchasers of care outside the locality, at the expense of local people?'

The second major change proposed is that of opt-out doctors. Despite the absence of the conditions normally regarded as necessary for the operation of a market — informed, leisured choice by consumers, clearly indicated quality and costs from suppliers, etc. — in the field of health care, the aim is to set up a market within the NHS, with the GPs as the agents for patients, buying services from hospitals depending on their cost and availability. Only the largest 9% of practices will at first be offered such budgets. Again, the patients with poorest health are likely to face discrimination and, as the National Association of Health Authorities states, 'If its proposals on GP budgets are to work then this will necessarily reduce referral freedom. GP non-budget holders will also be affected.'

Further steps along the road to eventual completely private medicine are likely to follow, so undermining the principle of access to health care regardless of means and opening the door to the kind of patient-led cost escalation seen most vividly in America.

Meantime, the most conspicuous feature of the Health Service review is the absence of any commitment to new resources. A few new consultant posts have been promised. The waiting list initiative has continued. A computer information system has been approved, not because it is long overdue but because it is an essential prerequisite of the trading arrangements now under construction. The government's greatest enthusiasm is for private medical insurance tax reliefs for which, in marked contrast with the funding of the public sector, no budgetary limit has been set.

For general health care, open to all, no new resources are on offer. As we end the Eighties, the twin Tory themes of ten years' health politics — the slow strangulation of the NHS by underfunding and the persistent, uneconomic and dogmatic pursuit of private sector answers to the problems thus created — dominate the scene as never before.

14

The Enemy Within

'Liberty is ill in Britain.'

Ronald Dworkin

After ten years of Mrs Thatcher Britain is not a fairer society, nor is it any more free. The government that boasts of having rolled back the frontiers of the state has in fact diminished many of the rights of its citizens. In the last year alone, in the name of national security, the media have been censored — with the broadcasting ban on interviewing Sinn Fein — and the right to a public interest defence in any official secrets case has been removed. Government employees, denied their right to membership of a trade union, have been sacked from GCHQ at Cheltenham.

No one should have been surprised. Earlier than 1986 the government sought to ban the book *Spycatcher* and its contents, even to the extent of impounding the English language edition of the newspaper *Pravda*. And, during 1987 the police raided the offices of the *New Statesman* and those of the BBC in connection with attempts to suppress a programme about the Zircon spy satellite.

In 1989 ministers are imposing the poll tax, football supporters' identity cards and a new and more restrictive Official Secrets Act. One writer has talked of 'the greatest ever peacetime controls of broadcasting' and another has described Britain under Mrs Thatcher as enduring the 'equivalent to a peacetime state of emergency'. For the first time in our history a special issue of the publication *Censorship* has been devoted to Britain.

The theorist Ronald Dworkin has argued that 'the sad truth is that the concept of liberty . . . is being challenged and undermined by the Thatcher government'. The recently formed rights organisation,

Charter 88, comprising people of all parties and none, has noted how 'the intensification of authoritarian rule in the UK has only recently begun'. The European Court of Human Rights now sees 800 complaints a year from UK citizens, more than from those of any other country. One decision in every three made in that Court is made against the British government.

As the state has claimed more power the individual has seen his or her rights progressively eroded. The government that has made so much of setting the people free has claimed new powers at their expense. Under Mrs Thatcher Britain is a more centralised state than ever before, more centralised than Germany, Italy, America or even France. A flat rate poll tax has been imposed. Control over local government has been increased and intermediate tiers — the Greater London Council and the Metropolitan Authorities — have been abolished. The legitimate aspirations of the Scots for an Assembly have also been denied. The Education Secretary has awarded himself 415 new powers, the Environment Secretary 350 new powers in relation to local government, with 100 over local housing for good measure.

Dworkin's argument that 'liberty is ill in Britain' rests on two propositions: that liberty of speech, information and conviction, which figure among fundamental human rights, have been diminished, and that there has been the growth of a culture less amenable to liberty. And as the Charter 88 organisation puts it, 'We have been brought up in Britain to believe that we are free, that our Parliament is the mother of democracy, that our liberty is the envy of the world, that our system of justice is always fair, that the guardians of our safety, the police and the security services, are subject to democratic legal control, that our civil service is impartial, that our cities and communities maintain a proud identity, that our press is brave and honest. Today such beliefs are increasingly implausible. The gap between reality and the received ideas of Britain's "unwritten constitution" has widened to a degree that many find hard to endure.'

As the Charter suggests, we have a government that seeks to impose its values on the civil service, to menace the independence of broadcasting, to threaten academic freedom in the universities and schools, to tolerate abuses committed in the name of national security. 'The break with the immediate past shows how vulnerable Britain has always been to elective dictatorship. The consequence is that today the British have fewer legal rights and less democracy than many other Western Europeans.'

There have of course been some advances for civil rights. Corporal punishment has been abolished in the state schools. A prisoner's right of access to his lawyer has been extended. Some interrogation techniques, such as sleep deprivation, used in Northern Ireland, have been banned. Contempt laws have been amended. Homosexuality has been legalised in Northern Ireland. But each of these improvements is the direct result of intervention by the European Court.

As a result of its judgements 80 British laws or regulations have had to be amended. Yet even the European Court has been unable to ensure the advances in civil rights made in other countries over the last ten years. Free assembly and free association are, for example, limited by the Conservatives because of 'the interests of national security or public safety', and as a result no action was taken by the European Court against blacklisting by MI5 or against the ban on trade unionism at GCHQ.

So what has happened to civil rights over these ten years? First, the government has been prepared to allow the erosion of such basic rights as the well established rights to free association and free expression. Secondly, the state has increased its powers at the expense of the individual and strengthened the power of its officials without any real increase in their accountability. Thirdly, although less tangibly, a new atmosphere of intolerance, characterised by prejudice and discrimination — against immigrants, against blacks, against other minorities — has developed.

This new intolerance is characterised in a McCarthyite phrase of the Prime Minister's own, when she spoke of 'the enemies within'. It is as though citizenship is no longer enough. In one famous speech Mrs Thatcher spoke of her ideal that every person should be 'a freeholder', ('There is no prouder word in our history than freeholder') suggesting that basic rights are somehow dependent upon the possession of property. It can be seriously contended that today's Conservatives take our basic freedoms less seriously because to them the main freedom is the freedom to make and retain money. In Mrs Thatcher's Britain there are a range of rights and freedoms to which people are not born; by means of a combination of possessions and approval, they buy them.

There is no Bill of Rights, or better provision for basic individual rights. There is not even a right to privacy. Instead there are fears that the government is prepared, as in the cases of *Spycatcher* and Zircon, to use censorship to control the free flow of information, secrecy to protect the confidentiality of decisions that should rightly be public and national security as a pretext for invading and searching offices and private dwellings. In addition to the absurdities of *Spycatcher* and the use of the Special Branch in impounding BBC property in connection with the Zircon programme, the government banned another serious and entirely responsible programme on the security services, *My Country Right or Wrong*, even though the secretary of the 'D' notice committee had agreed to be interviewed for it, and banned broadcast interviews with Sinn Fein politicians.

The *Spycatcher* affair did not establish any right of the citizen to free information, nor did it establish that the public had a right to know even if the secret services were in breach of the law. It did, however, demonstrate the enormous lengths to which the government was prepared to go to restrict the dissemination of official information. Having ruled out the possibility of prosecuting its author, Mr Peter Wright, under the Official Secrets Act in Britain, ministers took the remarkable step of seeking to ban publication via the Australian courts.

Attempts were made to prevent newspaper publication, culminating in the spectacle of 10,000 copies of *Pravda* being prevented from coming into Britain, a turn of events which must have brought joy to the hearts of its publishers in Moscow. The civil servant in charge of the government case assured himself a place in history when in court he admitted to being 'economical with the truth'.

In the Wright case the author and the media argued that the secret services ought to operate within the law and that it was in the public interest to know whether they did or not. But when the final judgement was delivered the Law Lords did not come to the defence of free speech or the freedom of the press in allowing publication. They concluded only that *Spycatcher* and its contents were now irretrievably in the public domain, their secrecy destroyed, and that formal publication would occasion no further damage. Government ministers could still claim that as a result of the case they had established the principle of a duty of confidentiality.

The *Spycatcher* affair had strong elements of farce. Little such light relief was evident in the government's handling of the TV documentary on Zircon and the radio series *My Country Right or Wrong*. In the former case a raid on the BBC's Glasgow offices brought echoes of Eastern Europe, in the latter the government was seen to take action against programmes containing interviews with former Defence Secretaries, former Home Secretaries and a former Lord Chancellor. The original injunction, modified a week later after public pressure, sought to ban the BBC from broadcasting any programme containing interviews with members of the security and intelligence services, past members included, or using any material obtained from them. We were not at war, but a serious documentary on a matter of public interest and national importance was assaulted with unnecessary and far-reaching legal force.

The programmes were eventually broadcast, but more lasting government interference with broadcasting was seen in the ban on coverage of the IRA. By preventing the BBC and the IBA from broadcasting interviews with members or supporters of Sinn Fein and other organisations the government handed the terrorists a powerful propaganda weapon, later enhanced by a conditional ban on Sinn Fein candidates and the removal of the British equivalent of the Fifth Amendment.

Perhaps most revealing of the underlying attitudes of government to broadcasting freedom was the conduct of a Home Office minister, Mr Timothy Renton, who told the broadcasting authorities to telephone the Home Office for instructions if they were in any doubt as to what they could or could not broadcast. As the Home Secretary, Mr Douglas Hurd, explained, 'This is not censorship because it does not deal with or prohibit the reporting of events. It deals with and prohibits direct access and its extra impact on terrorism and its supporters.'

Not censorship, but best ring us to be sure. And TV and radio can still report what Sinn Fein politicians say provided they cannot be heard or seen saying it. The ruling is at once clumsy, authoritarian, ineffectual and, because of the terrorists' propaganda gain, counter-productive. One of the few enthusiasts was Mr Botha, who declared that he would now be justified in introducing similar measures in South Africa.

The reform of the Official Secrets Act, long advocated by men and women of all parties, has in the event proved to be a step backwards rather than forward. Under the Act there is a new distinction between areas of public policy where there is a duty of confidentiality and where one cannot be justified. There are now six categories of official information which cannot be disclosed: security and intelligence, defence, international relations, information obtained in confidence from foreign governments and international organisations, information useful to criminals and interception of communications.

There is no freedom of information as such, and the most pernicious aspect of the new legislation is that it does not permit a general defence of disclosure in the public interest. As Mr Hurd stated in July 1988, 'It is not a defence to any other offence that the wider or long-term effects of the criminal act are beneficial and that the benefit outweighs the harm done.' In any future court action it could not be argued that information had been disclosed because, as Clive Ponting and Sarah Tisdall argued, parliament had been misled, or that fraud or other illegal activities had occurred.

The Peter Wright defence, that the information in question was already public, could not be used again. Nor has secrecy been diminished by the new security services legislation. Although this puts MI5 on a statutory footing, under the Home Secretary, for the first time, the Bill legalises bugging, telephone tapping and burglary where authorised, does not mention the existence of MI6 even though it costs £100 million or so a year, and does not provide any means of effective remedy for individuals who have complaints against the security services.

There is no right to privacy, or anything approaching it, in Britain. An estimated 30,000 telephones are tapped. According to *The Observer*, the numbers have risen dramatically during the Thatcher years and the numbers of British Telecom engineers engaged in tapping has risen by 50%. Under the Interception of Communications Act of 1985 the Home Secretary can grant a tapping warrant if he believes it to be in the interests of national security, or to prevent crime, or — blanket contingency — 'to safeguard the economic well-being of the United Kingdom'. And technical advances have weakened the protection of the law on telephone privacy since new equipment allows tapping without the physical presence of a specific device, thus eliminating the necessity for a warrant.

Information on individuals is now compiled and held on an unprecedented scale, and no proper right of redress exists. That information may be inaccurate or improperly disclosed but there is little the offended individual can do. Many are concerned by the huge amount of unchecked information held on the Police National Computer, and there is widespread and proper anxiety about the practice of blacklisting. A 1987 *World in Action* programme revealed how, as a result of the use of files held on trade unionists by the Economic League, men and women were denied jobs because potential employers had been given often inaccurate information. Recently it has been reported that the Economic League now intends to keep files on environmental activists too.

The implementation of the Poll Tax legislation shows how far ministers are now prepared to go in sanctioning intrusions into established liberties. To make the Poll Tax work, Poll Tax staff have the right to search through local government records and other sources of information, and a Poll Tax identifier will follow eligible adults in records throughout the country. Private agencies will also be involved in passing information around. Not surprisingly, the Data Protection Registrar has warned the government that there may be a conflict between the implementation of the Poll Tax legislation and the individual's right to privacy.

There has been little in the way of compensating increase in the protection of privacy over the last ten years. While in theory individuals have access under the Data Protection Act to all information held about them, the practical advantages are much more limited. There is no right of access to manual files, and only a restricted right to some types of computer-held information. And according to the Freedom of Information campaign many people will be deterred from applying to see their records simply by the cost.

Britain is significantly further from having a free press. The Monopolies Commission did not intervene when *The Times* and then *Today* were taken over by the Murdoch empire and only belatedly has an inquiry begun. Ten companies control most of our newspaper industry. The same degree of concentration is likely in television in the years to come if, as some Tories propose, public service broadcasting is to become a thing of the past.

Broadcasters are under attack on all fronts, prevented by government diktat from screening programmes labelled detrimental to the interests of the state, and forced by government pressure to eschew standards in the interests of free market ideology. Under the guise of deregulation, Mrs Thatcher's government has probably taken the decisions about broadcasting in Britain that will culminate in the abandonment of the concept of public service in broadcasting. The 'highest bidder' principle for TV franchises, central to the kind of deregulation which has already gone hopelessly wrong in Italy, will mean a reduction in programme quality and in the coverage of current affairs, in children's and minority interest programmes. Standards generally will suffer. While the government contends that its broadcasting policies will result in the development of new services responding to market demands, it is more likely that programme choice and quality will be dominated by a few vested interests, with the government holding back from any assertion on standards or of the public interest. A great tradition will have rapidly been destroyed.

The right of assembly and the right to protest have been curtailed in ways that were not contemplated under any other post-war Conservative administration. The 1986 Public Order Act requires advance notice of all moving demonstrations on pain of criminal prosecution and allows the police great discretion in imposing restrictions on any march or demonstration. Open air meetings of 20 or more can be banned. In this area, and in the powers of detention (and in the case of Northern Ireland the power to detain and enforce internal exile — 6,000 have been detained and interviewed and 275 have been excluded from mainland Britain) the influence of the police and the security services has been substantially increased, without any commensurate extension of their accountability.

But the government has done more to curb individual liberty than could have been achieved by legislation alone. It has created in Britain a climate of intolerance. Discrimination against women and the inadequacies of sex discrimination legislation are discussed in another chapter. Discrimination against homosexuals has received official encouragement in the form of the imposition of Clause 26 of the Local Government Act, which may prevent teachers informing young people about any homosexual issues.

Racial discrimination and intolerance is widespread, with the Commission for Racial Equality now worried that Britain could be subject to more inner city riots. According to the Runnymede Trust black workers are no better off now than they were when the first Race Relations Act came into force 20 years ago. Black people are twice as likely to be unemployed, often subject to bias in job selection, less protected in practice from discrimination by ignorance and anomalies in current Race Relations legislation, and more likely to be stopped by the police (of whom less than 1% are recruited from the racial minorities) even if never charged.

In 1987 the Social Science Research Council reported that 'the over-whelming majority' of young white people displayed racially prejudiced attitudes. Yet despite pressure from 1985 onwards from the Commission for Racial Equality urging reform of the Race Relations Act, to include greater help for individuals complaining to tribunals and more effective monitoring of equal opportunities policies, the government has refused to take any action.

Immigration laws have been tightened to exclude many categories of applicant previously admitted, in line with Mrs Thatcher's prejudice that Britain was in danger of being 'swamped'. The numbers accepted annually for settlement have fallen by one-third, from 69,670 in 1979 to 45,980 in 1987. Numbers from the Indian subcontinent have fallen even more sharply. The Nationality Act of 1981 and the Immigration Act of 1988 have almost completely stopped the entry of males from the Indian subcontinent to the UK.

The numbers who apply for asylum, around 3,700 a year, are less than in all comparable countries in Europe, not least because of an anomalous requirement that for entry into Britain refugees must first obtain documentation from the authority which is persecuting them. Numbers of applicants are low and the numbers accepted have actually fallen. When this, the harsh immigration laws, and the UK's current poor record on controlling racial discrimination are considered, it is easier to understand why there is anger in many of our communities.

Even in the areas of rights at work — where the Tories have presented themselves as the champion of the trade unionist against the trade union leader, much of the legislation has been designed in practise to shift the balance of power from trade unionists to employer.

Step by step over the last ten years the government has made the British worker more vulnerable to arbitrary and unfair treatment than at any time since 1945, and more exposed to such abuses than workers in most other countries in Europe. The underlying objective, that of giving employers a free hand, has not even succeeded in being universally welcomed by the employers.

The Eighties have certainly witnessed many explosions in industrial relations — the miners' strike, the events at Wapping, the Eddie Shah dispute — but in the main British industry and trade unions have sought to work in harmony. The balance of evidence is that trade unions help productivity, encourage efficiency, prevent large turnover in labour and make for better performance by management.

The experience of the last decade is that industrialists want better industrial relations based on consensus and agreements, not on conflict. Recent studies have shown that only one plant in five had made any real change in bargaining arrangements in the Eighties, that five-sixths of manual workers in private manufacturing had their pay determined by collective bargaining, that the number of shop stewards actually increased during the 1980s and that personnel management has become more, not less important to companies.

As one academic has written after a survey of the Eighties, 'managements in large firms have not been engaged in a systematic attack on the unions', and as the industrial relations director of Ford UK has said, 'in many areas of industrial relations the law was irrelevant, having more to do with political exigencies and public opinion than with industrial reality'.

Yet the government has insisted on changing the balance of power between worker and employer. Since 1979 several basic rights have disappeared or been eroded: the right to a fair wage, the right to equal opportunities and to maternity leave, and rights to safety at work, to a say in decisions at work and to be protected against unfair dismissal. After the repeal of the Fair Wages Resolution of 1891, and with the Wages Council legislation of 1906 to go later this year, there is no right to fair pay at work: changes that were made despite the findings of research commissioned from Cambridge University that showed no evidence that employment would increase if wages fell.

Today thousands more are subject to dismissal without any right to compensation. Protection against unfair dismissal used to commence after six months of service. Now two years of continuous service are required for protection. Now too the burden of proof has been removed from employers and there are proposals to make workers pay substantial amounts to bring a tribunal case in the first place. By the mid-Eighties tribunal applications claiming unfair dismissal were only half as likely to be successful as they had been in the mid-Seventies. Yet there is no significant research that shows employment protection rights to be a significant deterrent to employers in taking on workers.

Health and safety at work have suffered too. Since 1979 the incidence of major injury in manufacturing has risen by 25% and that in the construction industry by 42%. Yet since 1979 the staff of the Health and Safety Executive has been cut by 25%. And with the growth of small firms many more inspectors would be required simply to maintain the previous levels of supervision.

Women at work have done especially badly, thousands of women returning after maternity no longer have the automatic right to their old job. Women working for small employers no longer have a secure right to return at all. Women still earn less than men, the UK differential now being greater than that in any other European country except Spain and Portugal. Nowhere in Europe are provisions for child care poorer. And the women who form a majority of the part-time workforce must work for up to five years before they gain maternity, unfair dismissal and other rights.

The government has blocked every attempt to give employees the right to consultation over business plans that would alter their working lives, lobbying against each European measure intended to promote this. In 1983 ministers vetoed the Vredeling Directive on employee participation, which aimed to give modest consultation rights to workers, arguing that it 'failed the key test of whether it would help to create jobs'. In Europe employees are enjoying increased rights of participation over issues such as new technology. In Denmark employees are brought into discussions on the response to technological change, with cooperation committees established in the workplace. In Sweden there are technology agreements as well as joint discussions on efficiency and participation, in Norway a central agreement on technological change, and in Germany and France far more consultation than takes place in the UK.

But no single example illustrates better the government's disdain for basic rights than its decision to ban trade unions at GCHQ. It is the first time in our modern history that government employees have been sacked for belonging to a trade union. Now all of the last 18 trade unionists who defied the government have been transferred or dismissed. But other groups, like teachers, have already lost their rights to negotiate, and, under the Trades Union Acts of 1980, 1982, 1984 and 1988 traditional rights to assemble, to picket and to provide sympathetic support to fellow workers have been diminished to the point that, in many cases, they are far more limited than in other comparable democracies in Europe. But many changes made on the pretext that they were to award new rights to individual trade unionists have, in fact, been designed to benefit the employer in any conflict with trade unionists. In the 1984 law on pre-strike ballots, for example, it is the employer, not an individual trade unionist, who is given real power to take action against the trade union.

Under the current government, trade unionists - whether they be miners, print workers or even nurses — have been singled out as 'the enemy within'. They join individuals like Sarah Tisdall and Clive Ponting, investigative journalists, councillors, even on some occasions churchmen, as people to be denigrated by government propagandists.

It is hard to escape the conclusion that Britain is a more intolerant, less free, and more centralised state now than it was in 1979. As rights have been eroded, intermediate institutions have been abolished or seen their powers reduced. The abolition of the Greater London Council and the Metropolitan Authorities, and the reduction in local government powers everywhere, leaves democracy weaker in England and Wales. In Scotland the denial of democracy is even more keenly felt. Having refused Scotland an Assembly which a majority had voted for in 1979, government ministers have proceeded to scrap the Select Committee on Scottish Affairs — the one committee that monitors government decision making in Scotland — and subordinated much of Scottish legislation, tagging it on as subsidiary clauses in English legislation.

Ministerial responses to Scottish issues reveal a government that has increasingly refused to listen, even to the extent of reneging on past promises to the electorate. During the 1979 referendum the Conservative Party promised that they would bring forward further and improved proposals for devolution. 'A No vote would not mean the end to devolution,' Mrs Thatcher said. The official Conservative leaflet promised a constitutional conference to discuss four devolution options. The party chairman promised that a better 'house' would be constructed. The 1979 Conservative Manifesto promised all-party talks on devolution. One proposal was to strengthen the Select Committee on Scottish Affairs, a committee the Conservatives later abolished in its entirety. With a Scottish Assembly there would have been no Poll Tax, no opt-out schools or opt-out hospitals, and no buses or electricity privatisation. Nowhere is the denial of democracy more obvious than in the case of Scotland. Nowhere is the response of the majority of people — and their support for elementary democratic rights — now more clear.